ADAM SMITH

ADAM SMITH

and the pursuit of perfect liberty

James Buchan

P

PROFILE BOOKS

First published in Great Britain in 2006 by
Profile Books Ltd
3A Exmouth House
Pine Street
Exmouth Market
London EC1R 0JH
www.profilebooks.com

1 3 5 7 9 10 8 6 4 2

Printed and bound in Great Britain by
Clays, Bungay, Suffolk

A CIP catalogue record for this book is available from the British Library.

ISBN-10: 1 86197 905 3
ISBN-13: 978 1 86197 905 6

Contents

Abbreviations and References

Works of Adam Smith

The Glasgow Edition of the Works and Correspondence of Adam Smith, Oxford, 1976–87

TMS	*The Theory of Moral Sentiments*, ed. D. D. Raphael and A. L. Macfie, 1976
'Languages'	'Considerations Concerning the First Formation of Languages'
WN	*An Inquiry into the Nature and Causes of the Wealth of Nations*, ed. R. H. Campbell, A. S. Skinner and W. B. Todd, 1976
EPS	*Essays on Philosophical Subjects*, ed. W. P. D. Wightman, J. C. Bryce and I. S. Ross, 1980
'Ancient Logics'	'The History of the Ancient Logics and Metaphysics'
'Ancient Physics'	'The History of the Ancient Physics'

'Astronomy'	'The History of Astronomy'
'English and Italian Verses'	'Of the Affinity between Certain English and Italian Verses'
'External Senses'	'Of the External Senses'
'Imitative Arts'	'Of the Nature of that Imitation which takes place in what are called "The Imitative Arts"'
'Music'	'Of the Affinity between Music, Dancing, and Poetry'
Stewart, 'Life of Smith'	'Account of the Life and Writings of Adam Smith, LL.D.'
LRBL	*Lectures on Rhetoric and Belles Lettres*, ed. J. C. Bryce, 1983
LJ	*Lectures on Jurisprudence*, ed. R. L. Meek, D. D. Raphael and P. G. Stein, 1978
Corr	*Correspondence of Adam Smith*, ed. E. C. Mossner and I. S. Ross, 1987

Other Works

Carlyle, *Autobiography*	*The Autobiography of Dr Alexander Carlyle of Inveresk 1722–1805*, ed. J. H. Burton, Edinburgh, 1910
Ferguson, *Civil Society*	Adam Ferguson, *An Essay on the History of Civil Society*, ed. F. Ox-Salzberger, Cambridge, 1995
Hume, *Letters*	*The Letters of David Hume*, ed. J. Y. T. Grieg, London, Oxford, 1932

Hume, 'My Own Life'   David Hume, *An Enquiry concerning Human Understanding*, ed. A. Flew, Chicago, 1988

Hume, *Treatise*   David Hume, *A Treatise of Human Nature*, ed. E. C. Mossner, London, 1985

Hutcheson, *Short Introduction*   Francis Hutcheson, *A Short Introduction to Moral Philosophy*, Glasgow, 1747

Hutcheson, *System*   Francis Hutcheson, *A System of Moral Philosophy*, Glasgow, 1755

Mandeville, *Fable*   Bernard Mandeville, *The Fable of the Bees: or Private Vices, Publick Benefits*, ed. F. B. Kaye, Oxford, 1924

Mossner, *Life of Hume*   E. C. Mossner, *The Life of David Hume*, Oxford, 1980

Rae, *Life*   John Rae, *Life of Adam Smith*, London, 1895

Ramsay, *Scotland and Scotsmen*   John Ramsay of Ochtertyre, *Scotland and Scotsmen in the Eighteenth Century*, Edinburgh and London, 1888

Ross, *Life*   I. S. Ross, *The Life of Adam Smith*, Oxford, 1995

Scott, *Student and Professor*   W. R. Scott, *Adam Smith as Student and Professor*, Glasgow, 1937

Steuart, *Inquiry*   Sir James Steuart, *An Inquiry into the Principles of Political Oeconomy*, ed. A. S. Skinner, Edinburgh and London, 1966

For Evelyn

Introduction

'But I meant (said he) to have done more'

On 6 February 2005, the town of Kirkcaldy in Scotland played host to one of the famous men of modern times, the chairman of the United States central bank or Federal Reserve, Alan Greenspan.

Greenspan, who in saving the US economy from its decennial excesses in the 1980s and 1990s enjoyed a reputation unequalled in modern finance, had come to the windy shore of pubs, chapels and housing schemes on the Firth of Forth to praise its most famous native, the philosopher Adam Smith.

In attendance, along with the Provost and bailies, was the British finance minister or Chancellor of the Exchequer, Gordon Brown. Brown had grown up in Kirkcaldy, where his father had been minister at the Presbyterian Church of St Bryce. He was Member of Parliament for the town. He had lately been promoting Adam Smith as the patron of his version of a reformed Scottish socialism, and hoped to win Greenspan to his cause.

In his seventeen years as governor of the US central bank, Chairman Greenspan had become famous for impenetrable or Delphic sayings, but in Kirkcaldy he was clear. He said that Adam Smith was 'a towering contributor to the development of the modern world' for his 'demonstration of the inherent stability and growth of what we now term free-market capitalism'. This stability and growth arises, Greenspan said, in a principle discovered by Smith and called the 'invisible hand'.

'One could hardly imagine,' Greenspan said, 'that today's awesome array of international transactions would produce the relative economic stability that we experience daily if they were not led by some international version of Smith's invisible hand.'[1]

Couldn't one?

The phrase 'invisible hand' occurs three times in the million-odd words of Adam Smith's that have come down to us, and on not one of those occasions does it have anything to do with free-market capitalism or awesome international transactions. One could with better justice claim that Moll Flanders, a resourceful whore in the fiction of Daniel Defoe who also uses the phrase 'invisible hand', is another towering contributor to the stability of international markets.[2] The progress of the great man and his flatterers to this unfashionable shore, and the little battle done there of vanity with ignorance, would have delighted Adam Smith. 'Great success in the world,' Smith once wrote, 'great authority over the sentiments and opinions of mankind, have very seldom been acquired without some degree of excessive self-admiration.'[3]

Adam Smith is a much fought-over philosopher. Now celebrated as the apostle of capitalism and the champion of *laissez faire* in its rational Anglo-Saxon character, Smith was admired by Tom Paine and the French revolutionaries, inspired Karl Marx and coined the contemptuous term 'a nation of shopkeepers'.[4] In his best-known book, *The Wealth of Nations,* he wrote that 'civil government ... is in reality instituted for the defence of the rich against the poor.'[5] In his lectures at Glasgow University to young men preparing for the Scottish Church, he coolly discussed the rights and wrongs of tyrannicide. Far from being a rationalist, he thought half the people of Edinburgh were mad without knowing it.[6]

A close reading of *The Wealth of Nations* and other good evidence shows that Adam Smith was no doctrinaire free trader. He approves certain monopolies and restraints on trade, export subsidies and restrictions, sumptuary laws, penal taxation, limits on the rate of interest and the issue of bank notes, compulsory qualifications for craftsmen, the pressing of merchant sailors and discrimination against Roman Catholics. He was expert at exploiting the system of nepotism then dominant in the administrations of Britain, India and North America. He believed that government should be involved not only in educating but in *entertaining* the public. The words *laisser faire* or *laissez faire* appear nowhere in his work. Though he deplored British commercial policy in Ireland, the Americas and India, he thought the solution was not independence for those countries, but federation with the mother country.[7]

Yet nor was he the precocious Leftist of Gordon Brown's imagination. Brown attributes to him the phrase 'the helping hand', a conjunction of words that does not occur even once in Adam Smith's writings.[8] Brown's passion for arranging 'the different members of a great society', with his baby bonds and tax credits and windfall taxes and enterprise summer-camps and gap years and garden flagpoles, has done more to erect what Smith called 'systems of preference and restraint' than any British finance minister of modern times.[9]

Now Adam Smith is not some pre-Socratic philosopher – Heraclitus, say, or Democritus of Abdera – who has left only enigmatic fragments in an extinct language. Smith was a solitary man but none the less published and carefully revised two long essays in philosophy, lucid to the point of redundancy. His executors collected a few shorter works. No Scotsman, except maybe R. L. Stevenson, has ever written so well in the ordinary prose of England and the United States.

Though he was a poor correspondent, Smith left a couple of hundred of his letters to his chief associates, notably his beloved friend David Hume. We have no fewer than four sets of students' longhand notes of his lectures at the University of Glasgow. We know which books he had in his library and, often, where they are now.[10] His entire written output has been edited by able scholars in Britain, Germany and North America and is available in cheap editions. We lack only his poetry.

We thus have a case of two Adam Smiths. One is cautious, voluminous, virtuous, qualified, liberal with a small 'l' and utterly disdained. One is brief, brash, Liberal with a large 'L', inaccurate, shady and one of the most famous men who ever lived. What has happened?

The vulgar answer is that Adam Smith fell among economists and politicians who constitute, more even than professional footballers, always the least-literate sections of English-speaking society. One illustrious British economist once boasted he had never opened *The Wealth of Nations*. Another had done so, but not *The Theory of Moral Senti-*

ments on the report that it contained some psychology. Adam Smith, it seems, had glimpses of the eternal economic truths of which these men were hereditary masters. To have heard the name of Smith was sufficient evidence of their urbanity. His books, now, were long and Scotch and close-printed. They were no more use to the modern economist and politician than sixpenny tracts of eighteenth-century medicine to a busy General Practitioner or MD.

A more polite answer is that a historic change in attitudes which Adam Smith helped inaugurate has misled men and women who have studied hard to remove any trace of history from their reasonings.

The world in which Adam Smith was writing was not a modern economy, but had as much to do with the Roman Empire as the age of Alan Greenspan and Gordon Brown. Neither economics nor capitalism existed as mental entities. Smith was brought up in a backward corner of an unmechanised world, where the steam engine had not yet been brought to bear on the textile industry let alone transportation, where wages were so low it was cheaper to knit stockings by hand than by machine, and where the entire annual import of corn could today be supplied by a single modern 1,000-acre farm managed by father and son.[11] Smith's estimate of British national income was a hundred million pounds sterling, or less than the revenues of a large London or New York department store.[12] His national debt would shame a modern municipality. Smith's industrial purview takes in pins, buttons and nails, fire-engines, wind- and water-mills, iron forges, coalmines, hardware, woollen cloth, tanned leather, small beer, grass and hay, butcher's meat, manure. Smith thought the most beneficial deployment of capital was in agriculture.

Out of the pages of *The Wealth of Nations* there loom the engines of an utterly vanished world. 'A broad-wheeled waggon,' Smith writes, 'attended by two men, and drawn by eight horses, in about six weeks time carries and brings back between London and Edinburgh near four ton weight of goods.'[13] What has this prehistoric vehicle to do with Greenspan's array of international transactions, the inherent stability of free-market capitalism or Brown's helping hand? For Smith, one of the very best Latinists of his age, manufacture meant what it said: made by hand. His notion of a factory was twenty employees and £1,000 in capital employed.[14]

Meanwhile, political categories have been reversed. Smith had no strong political allegiance, hated faction and had friends among Whigs, Tories and Jacobites. He was regarded as a man of liberal principle and republican tendency, though neither meant much in a country where three thousand voters represented a million and a half people. Smith's strongest characteristic, after his hypochondria and solitude, was probably his concern for the poorest sections of society.[15] Indeed, the economist Thomas Malthus accused Smith of confounding 'the wealth of a state' with the 'happiness of the lower classes of the people'.[16] Since eighteenth-century government was in thrall to the interests of merchants and landowners, the key to furthering the cause of the poor was not *more* government, as in the imagination of Gordon Brown, but much, much less.

Finally, there seems to have been some attempt by Smith's followers to muddle his message and to soften or mitigate his radicalism. Smith was fortunate in his age of relative mental liberty. The intense *theological* vigilance of the Scottish seventeenth century had abated by the 1750s when a campaign in Edinburgh to excommunicate Smith's mentors, Henry Home and David Hume, was voted down by the progressive ministers and laymen of the Scottish Church. Yet after the French Revolution of 1789, a new *political* vigilance destroyed Scottish liberal thought, possibly for ever. Already, like Hume before him, and for reasons of prudence, Smith had retreated from his advanced or exposed philosophical positions. In the last revisions to *The Theory of Moral Sentiments*, completed in 1789, Smith argued that a man of good will and public spirit 'will respect the established powers and privileges ... of the great orders and societies, into which the state is divided'.[17]

Almost all biographical knowledge of Smith derives from the eulogy delivered by Dugald Stewart, the liberal professor of moral philosophy at Edinburgh, to the Royal Society of Edinburgh on two evenings, 21 January and 18 March 1793. Stewart's performance took place in the shadow of the execution of the king in France and the Sedition trials of radicals in Edinburgh. In the most notorious of the Scottish trials, the lawyer Thomas Muir (who had studied at Glasgow under Smith's friend and pupil John Millar) was shipped to Australia for fourteen years for calling for political reform. In this hysterical atmosphere, Dugald Stewart wrote, 'all freedom both of speech and of the press has been suspended.'[18] Looking back in 1810, Stewart wrote that 'the doctrine of a Free Trade was itself represented as of a revolutionary tendency; and some who formerly prided themselves on their intimacy with Mr Smith, and on their zeal for the propagation of his liberal system, began to call in question the expediency of subjecting to the disputations of the philosophers, the arcana of State Policy, and the unfathomable wisdom of the feudal ages.'[19] While their elders raved against liberty and the people, the liberal lawyer Henry Cockburn remembered, the young men of Edinburgh 'lived upon' the late Commissioner of Customs Adam Smith.[20]

In his eulogy, Stewart devoted as little time to *The Wealth of Nations* as he could but could not quite ignore it. He conveyed the impression that political economy was a harmless, technical sort of subject and Smith an unworldly fellow. The printer William Smellie, who knew Smith less well, also promoted the idea of a man 'but ill qualified for the general intercourse of society'.[21] It is as if the chief Scottish memoirists of that time – the Revd Alexander Carlyle, John Ramsay of Ochtertyre,[22] Smellie, Henry Mackenzie and then, towering over them, Sir Walter Scott – conspired to create a sentimental and harmless old dodderer shuffling up the High Street, his cane on his shoulder. I will show in this short biography that, for all his old-fashioned manners, Smith was alert, practical, cautious, urbane and businesslike.

Adam Smith was aware that he was prone to the fault of the ancient philosopher Epicurus, which was 'the propensity to account for all appearances from as few principles as possible'.[23] Smith himself greatly distrusted statistics, and slept through the only lecture on political economy he is known to have attended, but that did not deter his economist successors. The complex pyschology of commercial society, which Smith had devoted his life to understanding, John Stuart Mill abolished. Political economy, he said, 'does not treat of the whole of man's nature as modified by the social state, nor of the whole conduct of man in society. It is concerned with him solely as a being who desires to possess wealth, and who is capable of judging of the comparative efficacy of means for obtaining that end. It predicts only such of the phenomena of the social state as take place in consequence of the pursuit of wealth. It makes entire abstraction of every other human passion or motive.'[24]

Mill promised he would produce a new *Wealth of Nations*, only better: 'adapted to the more extended knowledge and improved ideas of the present age'.[25] (Yes, sneered Karl Marx, and General — thinks he's the Duke of Wellington.[26]) Mill's work, *Principles of Political Economy*, was the chief literary education of economists till early in the twentieth century, when it was replaced by Alfred Marshall's *Principles of Economics*. If you believe that a science can be erected on a single abstraction, taken out of time and in isolation, then you are unlikely to derive much instruction from the concrete and historical matter in Smith's work. You will find *The Wealth of Nations*, as the Victorian economic journalist Walter Bagehot found it, merely 'a very amusing book about old times'.[27] Or, like Mill and Greenspan and Gordon Brown, you decide that it was yourself who wrote *The Wealth of Nations*.

Inspired by his reading of ancient philosophy, and by the achievements of the modern natural scientists such as Isaac Newton, Adam Smith sought to organise our experience of the world into a series of interlocking systems. Surveying the general order and, within limits, decency of modern Scottish social life, he thought he espied a guiding principle in the operations of what he called 'sympathy'; but in trying to bring this principle to bear on the government of society and its laws, he came to grief. Smith had a vision of some stupendous philosophy of science and the arts but it never proceeded beyond fragmentary essays.

Rebuffed from justice and knowledge, Smith began to inquire into the material conditions of people's lives and how they found their sustenance. In modern commercial society, he saw that there were mechanisms that distributed welfare more thoroughly than the slave economies of the ancient world or the Asian monarchies. Once again, he came up against limits to his system and he ended his life in a distress bordering on despondency. 'But I meant (said he) to have done more.'

This book is designed to draw Smith out of the mystifications of the economists and the simplifications of politicians and place him in view of the public. It employs no jargon, philosophical or economical. Its novelty, if it has any, lies in three directions. It will show that *The Theory of Moral Sentiments* is not only good philosophy and literature but even, in the modern sense in which that word is understood, good *economics*. It will restore to Smith's biography the primacy of feeling over reason. It will argue that those seeking to appropriate Adam Smith as a legendary founder of their ideologies, a sort of shady Romulus, do nobody a service.

1

Fatherless World

1723–1746

dam Smith once described his life as 'extremely uniform'.[1] The chief part of it he passed in masculine institutions: the universities of Glasgow and Oxford and the Scottish Customs Board. Smith was a private man, never married, lived with his mother. He came to London first in his late thirties, travelled abroad once and only to France and Geneva. India, Central Asia, America and Africa, about which he wrote with passion and authority, he knew only from books. Of the great philosophers of modern times, only Immanuel Kant was more sedentary.

Smith's writings tell another story. The hermit of Glasgow University and the Edinburgh Custom-house thought the Irish prostitutes in London were the most beautiful women in the British Empire by virtue of their diet of potatoes. He had seen a black

African dance and both men and women jump in fright on their chairs, a woman appear at a ball in fake jewels, a mariner descry a ship on the horizon, greyhounds course a hare. He had watched poor people wrap pennies in their handkerchiefs and throw them to a stage quack, and twist and turn their bodies in sympathy to keep aloft a dancer on a slack-rope. He had visited dye-works, pin-makers, brewers and distilleries, examined the workings of factory machines, admired clipped yews in a shopkeeper's kitchen garden, noted the strapping children playing about a military camp, envied the beggars lounging on the roadside in the sunshine.[2]

The Victorian economic journalist Walter Bagehot affected to be surprised that the supposed 'recluse' should be so much less abstract in his theorising than the worldly stockbroker-economist David Ricardo[3] (or, we might add, the Scotsman John Law of Lauriston, who for a few weeks was prime minister of France and owned what is now the US state of Arkansas). The truth is that there is drama in Smith's life but it is played out not in his actions but in his thoughts.

Adam Smith was born in the early summer of 1723 at Kirkcaldy, a small port across the estuary or Firth of Forth from Edinburgh, the ancient capital of Scotland. He was the posthumous son of Adam Smith, and of Margaret Douglas. Local legend was that he was born at a house in the High Street at the corner with Rose Street, and later moved with his mother to a three-storey gabled house that was pulled down in 1834 but is commemorated by a plaque on the wall of the present Clydesdale Bank.

He was baptised on 5 June 1723. His birth date places him right in the middle of the circle of Scotsmen known since the early twentieth century as the 'Scottish Enlightenment'. A protégé of the philosophers Henry Home (born in 1696) and David Hume (1711), he was friend and colleague to the literary critic Hugh Blair (1718), the historian William Robertson (1721), the sociologist Adam Ferguson (1723) and the natural scientists James Hutton (1726) and Joseph Black (1728). He had for pupil the liberal philosopher John Millar (1735).

Adam Smith's father had practised as an attorney in Edinburgh, served as private secretary to the Earl of Loudoun when he was Secretary of State at the time of the parliamentary Union of England and Scotland in 1707, and been appointed Comptroller of Customs at Kirkcaldy in 1714. In the primitive divide of Scots allegiances at that time, the Smiths belonged to the 'Whig' party, supporters of the Protestant faith, a constitutional or parliamentary monarchy under the House of Hanover and Union with England.

Ranged against them were the adherents of the old Roman Catholic Stuart princes displaced in favour of the Protestant Hanoverians. The 'Jacobites', as those people were known after the last Stuart King, James II, appealed to old Tory notions of divine-right monarchy and also to the deep (and, as it were, permanent) Scots resentment of its powerful neighbour across the River Tweed. The Jacobites staged insurrections in 1708, 1715 and 1719.

Smith never knew his father, who had died the winter before he was born, casting heaven knows what shadow over the growing boy. Sometimes the most important events of a life occur before it has begun. All we can say is that Adam Smith was to adopt his father's profession in middle age, enforcing some government restrictions on trade that he throught quite futile, while retaining a strong romantic attachment to the personality of the smuggler.[4] His closest friend, the philosopher David Hume, also never knew a father.

Scotland at that time was one of the most backward countries in Europe, feudal in nature, intolerant in its religion and poor to the point of indigence. Union with England had been the last throw of a delinquent Scots nobility which saw no future for itself in a world being carved up into trading cartels.

Union promised an opening into English colonial markets, but that was a long time a-coming. Adam Smith became a Unionist through and through. He concluded that Union with England had broken the tyranny of the oppressive Scots aristocracy, and he recommended the same treatment for Ireland and, for different reasons, India and North America.[5] Even so, the 'immediate effect' of Union, he wrote, 'was to hurt the interest of every single order of men in the country'. That included those towns in the east, such as Kirkcaldy. 'The trade they were acquainted with, that to France, Holland and the Baltic, was laid under new embarrassments which almost totally annihilated the two first and most important branches of it.'[6]

The town, then as now, consisted of a mile-long street hugging the shore. Daniel Defoe, the novelist and boosting journalist who made a tour of the unified country in 1724, spoke of 'considerable merchants' sending corn and linen to England and Holland, a shipyard, coal-pits and salt-pans.[7] The Scots gentry was then, as it is now, too poor to indulge in prejudices against trade and the professions. One of the principal men of the town was the builder William Adam, whose son Robert (1728) became world famous as an architect in the classical style, and was a childhood friend of Smith's. Another prominent business family were the Oswalds of Dunnikier, whose eldest son James (1715) was to rise in the British government and had a strong theoretical interest in commercial questions, including the division of labour.[8] In the neighbouring villages was a cottage industry of nail-making, and Adam may have watched the men at work for he talks of nails as currency in *The Wealth of Nations*.[9] Perhaps it was at this age that Adam made a close study of the behaviour of wild and domestic animals.[10]

Adam Smith had a severe and classical notion of landscape. The modern cult of wilderness and wild nature started by Edmund Burke and the Ossian *pastiches* passed him by. In writing about such commercial policies as the bounty on corn, he takes no account of their effect on natural creation. The great movement to fence common land and open fields in the second half of the century, which all but obliterated the medieval landscape of Britain, is mentioned only in as far as it improved rentals.

Smith describes a landscape three times in his published works and it is always the same one.[11] 'Lawns and woods, and arms of the sea, and distant mountains' which he describes in his philosophy of vision in the essay 'Of the External Senses' are the same 'immense landscape of lawns, and woods, and distant mountains' that shows the role of imagination in forming what we see in *The Theory of Moral Sentiments* and are echoed in 'arm of the sea or a ridge of high mountains' that symbolise restrictions on poor people in disposing of their labour in *The Wealth of Nations*.[12] That a single view could make such a profound impression, and to take on the character of a philosophical universal, it must surely have been seen by a child. Was it the view from the Smith family house in Kirkcaldy?

As an infant, according to Dugald Stewart, Adam was 'infirm and sickly'.[13] At the age of three, on a visit to Margaret's brother John Douglas at Strathenry just inland of the town, in one of those back-eddies or interruptions in the placid flow of his biography, Adam Smith was abducted by tinkers. The story, which was told to Dugald Stewart by one of the sons of the minister at Kirkcaldy, became circumstantial. According to John Rae, Smith's Victorian biographer, a gentleman arrived at the Douglas house to say that he had seen a tinker woman carrying a child 'crying piteously'. A search party came on her in Leslie Wood, at which she threw the little boy down and fled.[14] Thus, wrote Dugald Stewart, there was preserved to the world 'a genius, which was destined not only to extend the boundaries of science, but to enlighten and reform the commercial policy of Europe'.[15] More to the point, said Rae, Adam 'would have made, I fear, a poor gipsy'.[16]

At the age of seven or later, he was sturdy enough to attend the Burgh School in Hill Street, where he was taught the rudiments of Latin. The two-room schoolhouse, built by the Town Council in the year of Smith's birth, is still standing as a sort of model or exemplar of the 'little school'[17] that he thought indispensable to every parish and district for the education of the poor. Together with his friends, Smith saw general education not as a threat to the social order but as a means to stabilise it. He merely proposed that a little elementary 'geometry and mechanicks' would serve ordinary people better than Latin.

While David Hume recommended Eton College to his relations, Smith always despised the practice of sending boys away from home to what are still called public schools in Britain.[18] He must have been well treated by the master of the Burgh School, David Millar, for he became an exceptionally kind and conscientious teacher himself, and was strongly opposed to harsh discipline.[19]

From grammar school, Adam Smith passed, in 1737, to the University of Glasgow as a stage on the way to Oxford. He was fourteen, an age then considered well ripe for university.

For those who know Glasgow only in its industrial and post-industrial phases, it is hard to imagine just how beautiful the city was at that time, nestling on the broad River Clyde amid green hills, a few streets scattered about the College and the Cathedral. There were perhaps twenty thousand inhabitants. Defoe had in the 1720s called it 'one of the cleanliest, most beautiful, and best-built cities in Great Britain'.[20] At that time, the foreign trade of Great Britain, which had consisted since time out of mind of the export of domestic woollen cloth to the European continent, was giving way to the financing and re-export of the colonial produce of America and India such as cotton cloth, sugar and tobacco.

By 1737, the merchants of Glasgow were just beginning to open up the trade with the British colonies across the Atlantic, chiefly tobacco from Virginia and Maryland for the making of snuff. With foreign countries barred by the Navigation Acts of the previous century from importing directly from British possessions, Glasgow was on the way to becoming the European emporium for what Voltaire called 'the stinking powder from America for stuffing up our noses'.[21] Smith was to compute that five-sixths of the tobacco brought into Britain was destined for re-export.[22] If, as Dugald Stewart wrote, Smith converted the Glasgow merchants to free trade,[23] it was, as it were, only after they'd become rich from exploiting trade restrictions.

The 'College' of Glasgow was founded by papal order in the fifteenth century but gathered up in Scotland's tumultuous Protestant reformation a century later. Standing in the High Street below the Cathedral, it consisted of handsome and uncomfortable seventeenth-century buildings in the Renaissance Gothic style and held some three hundred or so students from the west of Scotland and northern Ireland, most of them destined for the Presbyterian ministry. By the 1730s, it was beginning to shed its intense sectarian atmosphere under the spell of a number of professors, liberal in both religion and politics, most notably Francis Hutcheson, who had a European reputation for his philosophy of benevolence. A handsome man, Hutcheson brought to his class at Glasgow a species of high-minded rapture that his young and uncouth pupils found irresistible. He lectured not in Latin, as his predecessor Gershom Carmichael, but in English.

Smith would have spent his time at Glasgow on more Latin, Greek, 'Logicks, Metaphysicks and Pneumaticks', and mathematics.[24] This course of study was less medieval than it sounds. Lecturers at Scottish universities in those days had to keep very well clear of heresy or Jacobitism but otherwise enjoyed quite a wide choice of subjects.

Hutcheson, his teacher of 'pneumaticks', had little time for the metaphysical niceties of what spirits were and weren't and devoted his hours to a broad system of moral philosophy. [25] That was not merely a discussion of what was right and what was wrong. By the eighteenth century, moral philosophy encompassed systematic thinking on marriage and the family, basic jurisprudence, primitive customs, the history of institutions, international relations, religion, population, aesthetics, ethics and what has come to be called political economy. Inspired by the natural scientists, Hutcheson and the other British moralists sought to pierce the veils of society to discover universal principles of human nature from which human beings formed their notions of good and evil, duty and merit.

Smith inherited from Hutcheson not merely an impatience with 'the subtleties and sophisms' of the 'cobweb science of Ontology'.[26] He was also profoundly influenced by his likes and aversions. A disciple of the English moralist Lord Shaftesbury, Hutcheson believed that there was a faculty in human beings that spontaneously responded to virtue as to beauty: that is, a sort of innate moral sense distinguishes good and evil as infallibly as an aesthetic sense distinguishes between the beautiful and the ugly.

Smith was all his life fascinated by aesthetics and why, as he put it in a lecture, alone of the animals man is 'possessed of such a nicety that the very colour of an object hurts him'.[27] Dispersed through his works are thoughts on music, dancing, poetry, drama and gardening which, as we shall see, he hoped to organise into a grand philosophical work. Hutcheson's moral theory had a more straightforward fate for it survives as the starting-point of *The Theory of Moral Sentiments*.

If moral judgements are spontaneous, even spasmodic, there is no time for religious dogma or even rational self-interest. Hutcheson was disgusted by moralities based on self-interest and particularly the beguiling and scurrilous philosophy of Bernard de Mandeville (1670–1733). Mandeville, a Dutch doctor resident in London, published a sixpenny verse squib in 1705 called *The Grumbling Hive* which he revised and expanded in 1714 as *The Fable of the Bees: or, Private Vices, Publick Virtues*. His chief argument was that all that was known as virtue arose from self-interest. Love of profit or praise, it did not matter as the consequences were for the best.

Mandeville's argument was not, as economists sometimes claimed, that all vices were a benefit to society, but rather that all public benefits arose from vices. Luxury, attacked by both ancients and moderns for sapping both the moral strength of the individual and the wealth of the country, actually set industry in motion and employed the armies of poor men and women indispensable to modern society. Mandeville wrote like a pimp and his blend of moral anarchy and gutter utilitarianism was a red rag to the Shaftesburians, and provoked the chivalrous Hutcheson to champion humanity's essential good nature.[28] Smith was to denounce Mandeville in the *Theory*, but he had already absorbed not only his doctrine of beneficial luxury, but also, and somewhere below his moral consciousness, odd little bits of unchaste Mandevillian language.

In his 'private' class, where he took his pupils at noon, Hutcheson lectured on the ancient school of philosophy known as the Stoics, after the colonnade or *stoa* where they had met in ancient Athens. Their thought, which influenced Smith in all his reasonings, was preserved in the writings of the Roman orator Cicero and the Roman emperor Marcus Aurelius, whose *Meditations* Hutcheson translated during Smith's period at Glasgow.[29] For the Stoics, the world is organised in such a way that all activities and propensities, selfish and unselfish, combine for the benefit of the whole.[30] Smith was well aware of the moral and commercial paradoxes arising from that doctrine – if all is for the best, why bother to do one thing, rather than another? Why not kill yourself? – but did not succeed in resolving them.

Above all, both Carmichael and Hutcheson taught the 'natural jurisprudence' of the seventeenth-century Protestant jurists Huigh de Groot, usually known as Grotius, and Samuel Pufendorf that all human beings had *natural* rights and those are evident to the reasonable mind and heart. As Grotius wrote in 1608, God 'had drawn up certain laws, engraved not on tablets or on bronze, but on the minds and hearts of every individual, where even the reluctant and obstinate must read them. These laws are binding alike on the highest and the lowest, and kings have no more power against them than ordinary people against the decrees of their rulers.'[31] Liberty was a matter not just of freedom of religion and security of body, but of unhampered choice of livelihood and commerce.

Certainly, Hutcheson sets civil limits to natural liberty that Smith was to discard, but his tendency is liberal, even radical. ''Tis plain,' Hutcheson told his students, 'each one has a natural right to exert his powers, according to his own judgement and inclination, for these purposes in all such industry, labour or amusements as are not hurtful to others in their persons or goods, while no more publick interests necessarily requires his labours or requires that his activities should be under the direction of others. This right we call *natural liberty*. Every man has a sense of this right.'[32] On the evidence of his lectures, published as *A Short Introduction to Moral Philosophy* (1747), and his *System of Moral Philosophy*, published after his death but written in the 1730s, Hutcheson dealt in class with the division of labour, private property, value, money, real and nominal prices, and the 'principal contracts of social life' such as interest and insurance.[33]

The old notion that there was some tension or contradiction between Smith's moral and economic philosophy – between the 'system of commercial politics, and those speculations of his earlier years, in which he aimed more professedly at the advancement of human improvement and happiness',[34] as Dugald Stewart put it – is unbiographical. *Das Adam Smith-Problem* is best left to German professors.

Smith was to call his beloved teacher the 'never to be forgotten Dr Hutcheson'.[35] Yet he also busied himself with mathematics and natural science.[36] He greatly admired the brilliant professor of mathematics at Glasgow, Robert Simson, and wrote a warm tribute to him in his final corrections to *The Theory of Moral Sentiments*.[37] That Smith's first philosophical essay concerned astronomy is owing to Robert Dick, the Glasgow professor of natural philosophy or what is now called natural science.

Oxford, in contrast, where Adam Smith went up on horseback on a valuable £40 Exhibition or bursary to Balliol College in 1740, was sunk to its withers in Jacobite sloth. The university was less well organised than Glasgow to accommodate the new learning. It is said that the fellows of Balliol had so little to do they used to stand in Broad Street to watch the passage of the London mail coach.[38] 'It will be his own fault,' Adam wrote to his guardian, William Smith, on 24 August, 'if anyone should endanger his health at Oxford by excessive study.'[39] The six Scots Exhibitioners at Balliol were unpopular for their poverty and Hanoverian allegiances.

Smith made no English friends at Oxford, and commemorates not one of his professors. No doubt he had Oxford in mind when he wrote in *The Wealth of Nations* of ancient universities as 'sanctuaries in which exploded systems and obsolete prejudices found shelter and protection, after they had been hunted out of every other corner of the world'.[40] He goes on to say modern learning had advanced first at poorer universities – by which he must have meant Glasgow and Edinburgh – where 'the teachers, depending upon their reputation for the greater part of their subsistence, were obliged to pay more attention to the current opinions of the world'.

As a professor himself, he worked his pupils hard and kept them short of money in the old Scots way, but he looked after them as if they had been his sons. The surviving letters to the Earl of Shelburne, who sent his younger son to study with Smith at Glasgow in 1759, show his meticulous attention and kindness. Smith once said that he knew no 'engagements ... so sacred as ... to serve the young people who are sent here to study'.[41] In a world based on nepotism and patronage, Smith took immense pains to help young men (and even his former servants) start on their careers.

At Oxford, we have the first signs of the depression or hypochondria that is the ruling principle of Smith's character. Smith despised physicians and apothecaries as he despised lawyers, but he collected medical tracts and his own diagnostics are baffling even by the standards of the eighteenth century. In a fragmentary letter of 29 November 1743, he told his mother: 'I am just recovered of a violent fit of laziness, which has confined me to my elbow chair these three months.'[42] By 2 July of the next year, he has fallen prey to 'inveterate scurvy and shaking in the head'.[43] Tar-water – which the philosopher Bishop Berkeley had made fashionable at Oxford that spring – 'perfectly' cured him. In fact, shaking of the head continued all his life and combined with his protruding teeth and absence of mind to convey to the more polished generation of Sir Walter Scott and his friends a bucolic, even clownish, character.

Smith's Exhibition destined him for the Church of England, but there is no reason to believe his religion was any stronger at that stage than later. What he did, according to Dugald Stewart, was to read. 'The study of human nature in all its branches,' says Stewart, 'more particularly of the political history of mankind ... he seems to have devoted himself almost entirely from the time of his removal to Oxford.'[44] Smith 'diversified his leisure hours by the less severe occupations of polite literature'.[45] He worked on translations from the French to improve his English style, and indeed Smith never shared David Hume's anxieties about Scottish diction.[46]

Both the lectures on literature he delivered at Glasgow, and the reading lists he made up for his pupils there, show just how deep was his knowledge of Greek and Latin. In his modest way, he seems to have been at least as good a scholar of the ancient languages as Dr Johnson. Cicero, Aristotle, Plato and Epictetus appear in his philosophical works as easily as Hume, Montesquieu and Voltaire. What Smith almost never quotes is Christian scripture.

According to Smith's modern editors, it was at Oxford that Smith laid the foundation, if he did not actually complete, the beautiful fragment of what he later called 'a great work which contains a history of the astronomical systems that were successively in fashion down to the time of Des Cartes'.[47] In the spring of 1773, during an intense attack of hypochondria, Smith asked Hume in the event of his death to read the essay and himself decide whether it 'might not be published as a fragment of an intended juvenile work'. As it turned out, Smith long outlived his friend and the essay was published as 'The History of Astronomy' by Smith's executors, the scientists James Hutton and Joseph Black, in the posthumous *Essays on Philosophical Subjects* of 1795.

What was this 'intended juvenile work'? In a letter of his old age, Smith told the duc de La Rochefoucauld – grandson of the cynical aphorist – that he had two great works 'upon the anvil', of which one was a 'sort of Philosophical History of all the different branches of Literature, of Philosophy, Poetry and Eloquence'.[48] Smith feared that that must fall prey to the 'indolence of old age'.[49] The assumption is that the 'Astronomy' and two yet more defective essays on ancient physics and ancient logics and metaphysics, which share the same preamble and were also published by Hutton and Black, are ruins of this stupendous project. Smith's lectures on language, rhetoric and literature, and some 'detached essays' he passed to his executors on the psychologies of vision and the plastic and performing arts, may be other materials towards the scheme.

The full title of the 'Astronomy' gives a clue to his intentions: *The Principles which lead and direct Philosophical Enquiries; illustrated by the History of Astronomy.* The preamble, which is repeated with the two ancient histories, shows that Smith's prime intention was not to provide a history of astronomy, though he covers the four 'systems' of Ptolemy, Copernicus, Descartes and Newton with some learning and precision. His interest is psychological.

For Adam Smith, as for David Hume in the generation before, we inhabit a reality that is not nature but fashioned by our hearts and imaginations within nature. For the two men, emotions – or what they called passions and sentiments – were more plausible sources of action than so-called reason, and more solid items of experience. The Age of Reason was, in Scotland at least, the Age of Feeling. Smith very much disliked what he called, in a letter to the great medical doctor William Cullen in 1774, 'the presumption that commonly attends [natural] science'.[50]

In the 'Astronomy', Smith says that he will examine the four cosmological systems not in 'their absurdity or probability, their agreement or inconsistency with truth and reality' but only in their fitness or not 'to sooth the imagination, and to render the theatre of nature a more coherent, and therefore a more magnificent spectacle, than otherwise it would have appeared to be.'[51] In other words, he is not examining the truth or not of any particular scientific discovery, but the sentiments that give rise to it.

These sentiments are surprise and wonder. Nature is a chaos of inexplicable and contradictory phenomena. Philosophy, by 'representing the invisible chains which bind together all these disjointed objects, endeavours to introduce order into this chaos of jarring and discordant appearances, to allay this tumult of the imagination, and to restore it, when it surveys the great revolutions of the universe, to that tone of tranquillity and composure, which is both most agreeable in itself, and most suitable to its nature.'[52]

The Newtonian system is simpler than its precursors, more coherent and more comprehensive, and, in this hedonistic philosophy, more *pleasant*, but it is no less imaginary than that of Ptolemy:

And even we, while we have been endeavouring to represent all philosophical systems as mere inventions of the imagination, to connect together the otherwise disjointed and discordant phaenomena of nature, have insensibly been drawn in, to make use of language expressing the connecting principles of this one, as if they were the real chains which Nature makes use of to bind together her several operations.[53]

By our very manner of talking about the world we convert the imaginary into the certain.[54]

Smith's editors, the natural scientists James Hutton and Joseph Black, were unhappy with his treatment of the divine Sir Isaac and in a note attempted to dismiss it. 'It must be viewed,' they wrote, 'not as a history or account of Sir Isaac Newton's astronomy, but chiefly as an additional illustration of those principles in the human mind which Mr Smith has pointed out to be the universal motives of philosophical researches.'[55]

Re-reading the 'Astronomy' in 1773, Smith had his own doubts: 'I begin to suspect myself that there is more refinement than solidity in some parts of it.' Yet it was the only one of his unpublished works that he wished Hume to preserve, apart from the toilsome manuscript of *The Wealth of Nations*. In fact, in the guise of a psychology of scientific discovery, the 'Astronomy' expresses a cast of thought which is distinctive of Smith's mind and, in the era of Einstein, modern.

It is humanity's spontaneous love of order, of what Smith called in the 'Ancient Physics' 'a coherent spectacle to the imagination',[56] which lies behind our passion not just for scientific investigation, but for improvements in technology, the law or political systems, for the science of cutting yew and holly hedges, known as topiary, for the arrangement of chairs in a room, even the collecting of toys.[57] 'It gives us a pleasure,' Smith told his pupils, 'to see the phaenomena which we reckoned the most unaccountable all deduced from some principle.'[58] Even imaginary or false principles, such as the four primordial elements of Earth, Air, Fire and Water of the ancients, have their function since 'they could enable mankind to think and talk with more coherence, concerning those general subjects, than without them they would have been capable of doing.'[59]

In our day, where tragedies and operas dramatise the thoughts of Alan Turing and Robert Oppenheimer, the notion that there be some motive to the scientific enterprise other than mere love of truth is no longer repellent. Albert Einstein himself insisted on the provisional character of scientific theory, including his own.

In the 'Astronomy', there is a fleeting apparition of the phrase that caught the imagination of economists and business people in the twentieth century: the invisible hand. In this its first avatar, the invisible hand is not a commercial mechanism, but a circumlocution for God. It was one of several such current in the progressive ecclesiastical circle of Smith's professors at Glasgow.[60] Exposed to alarming and inexplicable natural phenomena, the savage mind sees the actions of 'the invisible hand of Jupiter'.[61] For the moment, the invisible hand is a projection of the yearning for coherence on to some supreme agent, on a father in a fatherless world.

2

Cave, Tree, Fountain

1746–1759

Adam Smith left Oxford in the late summer of 1746 without prospect of employment and, it appears, never to return. As Dugald Stewart reported, Smith had no taste for the 'ecclessiastical profession'[1] for which he was supposed to have studied. It seems that for a while he thought of acting as tutor to a nobleman's son. His friend David Hume had served for a short time as tutor to the young Marquess of Annandale, but Rae says Smith's 'absent manner and bad address'[2] would have scared away My Lord and My Lady. (Actually, for all these stories of his unworldliness, Smith proved an excellent travelling tutor in the 1760s to the young Duke of Buccleuch.)

Scotland was still reverberating from the near-success of the Jacobite rebellion of 1745. Edinburgh was under a cloud for surrendering to the rebels without firing a shot. Prince Charles Edward Stuart escaped back to the Continent that September but other leading Jacobites were still hiding out in the heather. Adam Smith rode up to Kirkcaldy and rejoined the person who was always his chief attachment, his mother. On the shores of the Firth, in the three-storey house on the High Street with the crow-stepped gables, he is lost in his thoughts.

He reappears in 1748 and this time in print. Adam Smith's first published work is an unsigned preface to *Poems on Several Occasions*, a collection of verses by, of all people, the Jacobite poet William Hamilton of Bangour. A protégé of the philosopher-jurist Henry Home, Bangour had joined the cause of the exiled Stuarts. After Edinburgh fell in ludicrous circumstances to the rebels, Bangour welcomed Prince Charlie to the royal palace of Holyrood on 17 September 1745 and wrote a poem to celebrate the Jacobite victory at Prestonpans three days later.[3] He was now in exile in France. Henry Home no doubt wanted both to help 'poor Willie' and launch Adam Smith into print.

A Jacobite himself until the 1730s, Home had spent the rebellion quietly on his estate in the Borders, working on his *Essays upon Several Subjects Concerning British Antiquities*. An energetic, clever, coarse, domineering lawyer, thin as a board and beak-nosed, he became known as the 'Scottish Voltaire', though not to the French Voltaire, who could not stand him.[4] He was fond of young people, boys and girls, but only so long as they thought his thoughts.[5] When not pulling strings, Home indulged the Scots double-passion for metaphysics and agriculture, without quite succeeding at either. Even so, only David Hume dared to tease him.

Home gave Smith more lasting employment that year when he arranged for him to be invited to deliver a series of public lectures on rhetoric in the capital. These lectures were probably sponsored by the Philosophical Society of Edinburgh, which Home was trying to revive after the chaos and interruption of the 'Forty-five. Smith lectured that winter, and the two following, to an audience consisting of ambitious young men such as Alexander Wedderburn, later Lord Chancellor, and the critic Hugh Blair. The lectures brought him a clear £100 sterling a year for three years, or the same salary as at least one of the professors at the University.[6] They also ensured that when, in 1751, the chair of logic and rhetoric became vacant at Glasgow University, though he was just twenty-seven years old, Smith was the strongest candidate.

We have no copies or notes of the Edinburgh rhetoric lectures. A set of student's notes to lectures on literature at Glasgow in the winter of 1762–3 turned up at auction in Aberdeen in 1958.[7] How much Smith had changed his lectures since that first winter in Edinburgh is impossible to say. He had certainly brought them up to date: there are references in the student's notes to Thomas Gray's *Elegy* of 1751, Jean-Jacques Rousseau's *Discours sur l'inégalité* of 1755, and James MacPherson's pastiches of an ancient Celtic bard he called Ossian of the early 1760s. What can be said is that they are a glimpse of that phantom 'Philosophical History' of the sciences and arts that Smith was never to complete.

Rhetoric, or the science of persuasion, was as important in the eighteenth century as in our age of television and advertising. 'Speech is the great instrument of ambition,' Smith was to write, 'of real superiority, of leading and directing the judgments and conduct of other people.'[8] With no trade or industry to speak of in Edinburgh, and few inherited fortunes of any note, young Scotsmen sought distinction in professions that all required fluency in speaking or writing: the Courts, College and Kirk, the House of Commons, the military or, like James Boswell and Hume, the printing press. And they needed to make their way in an English-speaking world that was suspicious of the loyalty and goodwill of Scots and affected not to understand their accent. Henry Home, who had no college education himself, chose Smith not simply because he had read so much and so widely at Oxford but because he had learned there to speak English like a southerner.

As criticism, Smith's lectures stand in between the system of rules of the antique rhetoricians and the suite of spontaneous aesthetic responses understood under the eighteenth-century heading of 'taste'. Style, both in speaking and writing, must arise in the personality, and be delivered without affectation. 'When the sentiment of the speaker is expressed in a neat, clear, plain and clever manner, and the passion or affection he is possessed of and intends, *by sympathy*, to communicate to his hearer, is plainly and cleverly hit off, then and then only the expression has all the force and beauty that language can give it. It matters not the least whether the figures of speech are introduced or not.'[9]

Yet for all his discussion of Homer and Cicero, Swift and Shaftesbury, Smith was less interested in language as tool of professional advancement than as a window, even the main window, on how the mind works. If language was the 'characteristical faculty' of human nature, that no other animal possessed or employed, might it not also be the key to the other great human inventions, such as law or commerce or money? (In contrast, another quarrelsome Edinburgh philosopher-judge, Lord Monboddo, argued that language was not a necessary characteristic of human beings, and made himself a laughing stock by contending that orang-utans were human beings who had not attained the faculty of speech.[10])

For some time, Smith toyed with the notion of composing what he called a Rational Grammar of language for he believed it would offer 'the best history of the natural progress of the human mind in forming the most important abstractions upon which all reasoning depends'.[11] He criticised Dr Samuel Johnson's famous *English Dictionary* in 1755 for failing to do that.[12] He sought to investigate how the circumstances of society affected literary style and how, in the flourishing cities of the later Roman Empire, leisure gave rise to the sentimentality of the Roman historian Tacitus.[13] He recognised that there was an organic connexion between the rise of commerce and the use of prose as a medium of communication: that 'No one ever made a Bargain in verse.'[14] At this period, Smith was groping towards an idea of money itself as a tool of *persuasion* though – unfortunately for us – he abandoned that line of reasoning in the published version of *The Wealth of Nations*.[15]

The rhetoric lectures also throw a shaft of light over Smith's philosophical method. In the twenty-fourth lecture, Smith says there are two capital methods for presenting a philosophical system: 'either 1st we lay down one or a very few principles by which we explain the severall rules, or phaenomena, connecting one with the other in a natural order, or else we beginn with telling that we are to explain such and such things and for each advance a principle either different or the same with those which went before.' As might be expected, Smith very much prefers the first manner, which he associates with the natural science of Sir Isaac Newton, over the second or Aristotelian approach. 'The Newtonian method is undoubtedly the most philosophical – It gives us a pleasure to see the phaenomena which we reckoned the most unaccountable all deduced from some principle (commonly a wellknown one) and all united in one chain.'[16] Smith's masterpieces, *The Theory of Moral Sentiments* and *The Wealth of Nations*, both open with distinctive theories founded on 'wellknown' principles (sympathy, the division of labour) which are then deployed to marshal arrays of subsidiary social and commercial fact.

In a lecture that was published separately in 1761, as 'Considerations Concerning the First Formation of Languages, and the Different Genius of Original and Compounded Languages', Smith examines the forms of language to suggest how a process of mental abstraction might arise: how, for example, the adjective *green* came into being, or the notion of *greenness*. Smith was proud of this essay,[17] and with justice, for it is novel and clear as clean water. Dugald Stewart, in his eulogy of Smith before the Royal Society of Edinburgh, singled the essay out as an example of a modern scientific approach which 'seems, in a peculiar degree, to have interested Mr Smith's curiosity ... and may be traced in all his different works, whether moral, political, or literary'. To describe it he coined a term which is now well known, '*Theoretical or Conjectural History*'.[18]

The eighteenth century was confronted with stupendous mental artefacts whose origins and progress were lost: languages of great sophistication, intricate sciences and arts, forms of political organisation, principles of government and networks of kinship. It would no longer do to argue that history was a degeneration from Paradise, where distinctions of tongue and custom might be attributed to the Flood or the Tower of Babel. So how then had society in Europe progressed to its present sophistication and polish? How was it, in Walter Bagehot's sneer at this strand of Scottish thought, 'from being a savage, man rose to be Scotchman'.[19]

Facts were in short supply, either because of the primitive attainments of the new sciences of archaeology and philology or because, as Stewart put it with great understanding, 'long before that stage of society when men begin to think of recording their transactions, many of the most important steps of their progress have been made.'

The answer was to make it up. 'In this want of direct evidence,' Stewart said, 'we are under the necessity of supplying the place of fact by conjecture; and when we are unable to ascertain how men have actually conducted themselves upon particular occasions, of considering in what manner they are likely to have proceeded, from the principles of their nature, and the circumstances of their external situation.'[20] In Smith's case, 'whatever be the nature of his subject', he liked to trace its origin from 'the principles of human nature, or from the circumstances of society'.

Smith did not originate this theorising, nor, with respect to Dugald Stewart, was it modern. Tacitus and Aristotle are pioneers.[21] The Bordeaux jurist Charles de Secondat, baron de Montesquieu, in his *De l'Esprit des Lois* of 1748 investigated human laws and institutions not as if they were the legacy of heroic lawgivers (as in scripture and the ancient writers); nor as adventitious; but as moulded, in however mysterious a fashion, by the material circumstances of society, effects of soil and climate and region, commerce, custom and the passage of time. Modern Tartars and Hottentots and native Americans, in those manners and institutions described by the new breed of scientific traveller, offered tantalising glimpses of how European societies might have been at earlier stages of their formation.

This approach, which had no place for timeless notions of divine right or class privilege, had a powerful attraction to Scotsmen such as Henry Home, who gaily transferred Montesquieu's approach to the most crabbed Scots law in his *Historical Law Tracts* of 1758, to Sir John Dalrymple in his *Essay towards a General History of Feudal Property in Great Britain* (1757), and to John Millar in *Origin of the Distinction of Ranks* (1771). David Hume's cool and provocative anthropology of faith in his *Natural History of Religion* of 1757 offended many in the Scots and English churches and caused no end of trouble to his friends in Edinburgh and Glasgow. Smith combined observation of human nature and the material conditions of life to explain phenomena as diverse as the decay of the feudal system in Europe or the fall from fashion of hedge topiary.

The problem, as Dugald Stewart saw with great penetration, was the artificial character of this history. 'In most cases,' he wrote, 'it is of more importance to ascertain the progress that is most simple, than the progress that is most agreeable to fact; for, paradoxical as the proposition may appear, it is certainly true, that the real progress is not always the most natural.'[22] What the eighteenth century assumed to be nature is often mere conjecture concerning its constitution and history. Smith's account in his lecture of the origin of language, in which two cave-dwellers 'by mutual consent agree on certain signs' to distinguish their local cave, tree and fountain,[23] is considerably less convincing a linguistic theory than the Tower of Babel in Genesis. Likewise, Smith's bold accounts of the origin of song and verse in the 'Imitative Arts',[24] of scientific speculation in the 'Ancient Physics',[25] or of commerce in some fabulous Propensity to Truck at the beginning of *The Wealth of Nations*.[26] John Stuart Mill put it well when he wrote: 'What are called first principles are, in truth, last principles ... [for] they are the truths which are last arrived at.'[27]

At times, indeed, Smith explicitly prefers what he calls the natural to the actual, and devotes an entire book in *The Wealth of Nations* to comprehending and explaining why history has been so perverse and misbehaved. Governor Pownall, a bore of secular capacity and a great headache to Smith, none the less had some justice when he complained that amid all the theorising on the state of the American colonial trade in *The Wealth of Nations*, we might have been given an 'actual deduction of facts'.[28]

This cavalier approach to matters of fact made Smith and his circle vulnerable to the Ossian impostures in the 1760s and the ridicule of Dr Johnson and his friends in London. In a draft of *The Wealth of Nations*, Smith speaks of the world of Ossian as if it were historical.[29] The speculative habit survives in the social sciences that draw their inspiration from the Scottish school: history, sociology, anthropology, the study of language and political economy.

It was in Edinburgh at this period that Smith made the most important friendship of his life. David Hume had returned in 1749 from diplomatic missions to the Continent, fat, good-natured, a decent cook and a better eater, and the object of fascination to women and suspicion to the pious. His great philosophical *Treatise of Human Nature* of 1739–40 had failed – fallen 'dead-born from the press',[30] as he himself put it – but people understood enough of it to see that here was no field-preacher in homespun. When Hume stood as a candidate for the professorship of moral philosophy at Edinburgh in early 1745 he was blocked by the ministers of the town kirks. He was now living at his family estate at Ninewells in Berwickshire and recasting the cardinal principles of the unfortunate *Treatise* in the form of short, polite essays. To have chosen Hume as a friend showed Smith's boldness, while his prudence kept the older man at arm's length.

Adam Smith arrived in Glasgow to take up his post on 1 October 1751.[31] He lost no time in reminding the place of his dislike of old-fashioned scholastic learning. According to John Millar, 'he soon saw the necessity of ... directing the attention of his pupils to studies of a more interesting and useful nature than the logic and metaphysics of the schools [i.e. medieval philosophy].' The bulk of his time he dedicated to his Edinburgh 'system of rhetoric and belles lettres' as 'the best method of explaining and illustrating the various powers of the human mind'.[32]

Even before arriving in Glasgow, Smith had agreed to a request to take over the moral philosophy class, where Hutcheson's successor, Thomas Craigie, had fallen ill. On a suggestion conveyed by William Cullen, professor of medicine, Smith was to lecture on 'natural jurisprudence and politics' while poor Craigie went south for his health.

As it turned out, Craigie died at Lisbon in November and Smith was elected to his vacant chair the following April. No doubt that had been the intention of the Glasgow faculty all along. David Hume lobbied for the vacant chair of logic, but received a flea in his ear. 'I should prefer David Hume to any man for a colleague,' Smith had told Dr Cullen back in November. 'But I am afraid the public would not be of my opinion; and the interest of the society [i.e. college] will oblige us to have some regard to the opinion of the public.'[33] In that, Smith was surely right. Hume was opposed by the Glasgow Presbytery and received no support from the most powerful patron in western Scotland, the Duke of Argyll. Even at the Faculty of Advocates in Edinburgh, where he was appointed librarian in consolation, Hume soon blotted his copybook by ordering some racy French titles. If David knew of Smith's lack of enthusiasm, he forgave it. In a letter of September 1752, he asks Smith to look over his *Essays, Moral and Political* for a new edition and suggest anything to 'be inserted or retrench'd'.[34]

Smith was to teach moral philosophy at Glasgow for thirteen years, which he described as 'by far the most useful, and therefore as by far the happiest and most honourable period of my life'.[35] At first, his mother kept house for him and she was helped, at least from 1754,[36] by his unmarried cousin, Janet or Jean Douglas, of whom he became very fond. They moved house three times.

During those years, as his biographer W. R. Scott showed through his study of college papers in the 1930s, Smith was at the very heart of the administration of the university. He was entrusted with difficult legal and financial matters, the management of property, the library and building work. He wrote the speeches for ceremonial occasions and negotiated delicate university business in Edinburgh, London and Oxford. This was in a period where, as Rae put it, the ancient constitution of the university, with its separate government for University and Faculty, 'seemed to be framed as if on purpose, to create the greatest possible friction in its working'.[37] Smith was true to the principle, as he put it in a late revision to *The Theory of Moral Sentiments*, that 'the most sublime speculation of the contemplative philosopher can scarce compensate the neglect of the smallest active duty.'[38]

Glasgow University at that time was a good place for an inquiring mind. In one corner of the college, Dr Joseph Black, Cullen's successor as professor of medicine (and lecturer in chemistry), was working on chemical experiments that were to open up the use of alkalis in the glass, soap and bleaching trades, and identify and separate the gas now known as carbon dioxide. His experiments in heat and evaporation influenced the practical genius of the young James Watt. Born at nearby Greenock in 1736, Watt had trained as a maker of mathematical instruments but, since he had not served an apprenticeship in Glasgow itself, was barred by the corporations from trading there. Instead, he was taken on by Robert Dick in 1757 as the college instrument-maker, and in 1763 was asked to repair the college's small-scale model of Thomas Newcomen's primitive steam-engine. In one of the most famous of all scientific epiphanies, while walking on the College Green one Sunday, Watt realised that that the performance of the engine – which is still at the college – could be greatly improved if the steam could be drawn off and condensed back into water without cooling the cylinder. 'I had not walked farther than the Golf-house,' Watt remembered years later, 'when the whole thing was arranged in my mind.'[39]

Joseph Black became one of Smith's most intimate friends. Of Smith's dealings with Watt, there is less hard evidence. A College minute of 11 November 1762 records that Smith was appointed to a committee to reclaim some of the space now taken up by Watt and by the great printer Robert Foulis, then engaged in producing his sumptuous editions of the Greek and Latin classics.[40] At this time,

Smith was working at a theory of innovation. In the lectures and an early fragment of *The Wealth of Nations*, Smith contends that industrial innovation mostly arises in the field or on the factory floor; but that revolutionary processes, such as the steam-engine, or 'fire-engine' as it was then called, are the work of contemplative minds. 'It was a real philosopher only,' he writes in an early draft of Chapter Two of *The Wealth of Nations*, 'who could invent the fire engine, and first form the idea of producing so great an effect by a power in nature which had never before been thought of.'[41] Perhaps because that might distract from his theme of the division of labour, Smith confined himself in the published version of *The Wealth of Nations* to improvements made by specialised workmen. He tells how a boy, employed to open and shut a valve on a steam-engine as the piston moved, discovered that he could tie it in such a way that it opened and shut on its own, and he could be off with his friends.[42] Smith, who hated ever to use a pen, later paid six guineas for Watt's ingenious duplicating machine, patented in 1780.[43]

Out in the town, the colonial trade was expanding rapidly under the influence of the opening of the first banks, the Ship Bank in 1749, the Arms in 1750, and the Thistle in 1761. 'I have heard it asserted,' Smith wrote in *The Wealth of Nations*, 'that the trade of the city of Glasgow doubled in about fifteen years after the first erection of the banks there.'[44] According to Alexander Carlyle, who had been a student in Glasgow under Hutcheson, John Cochrane, one of the leading Virginia merchants and Lord Provost of Glasgow, had established as early as 1743 a club to 'inquire into the nature and principles of trade in all its branches'. He said that Smith was later a member and was indebted to Cochrane's 'information, when he was collecting materials for his *Wealth of Nations*'.[45] Smith also entertained the American scientist and statesman Benjamin Franklin, when he visited Glasgow in late 1759.

In his moral philosophy public class in the morning, Smith would have lectured to about eighty or ninety young men. He would have taken about twenty boys in his private class at noon. Most were destined for the Presbyterian ministry in Scotland or Ulster. John Millar, in a letter to Dugald Stewart quoted earlier in the chapter, said that Smith's lecture course was divided into four parts. The first covered natural theology, in which Smith looked at the 'proofs of the being and attributes of God', and more to his taste, 'those principles of the human mind upon which religion is founded'. Nothing is known of these lectures, which Stewart thought were burned just before Smith's death. John Ramsay of Ochtertyre reported that Smith asked to be excused from opening his class with a prayer, but was refused.[46]

The second part covered ethics, and consisted chiefly of the doctrines worked up into *The Theory of Moral Sentiments*.[47] The third part dealt with morality as it is codified into justice, and seems to have been based not just on the natural law theories of his student days in Glasgow but on the approach of Montesquieu: 'to trace the gradual progress of jurisprudence, both public and private, from the rudest to the most refined ages, and to point out the effects of those arts which contribute to subsistence, and the accumulation of property, in producing correspondent improvements or alterations in law and government'. The fourth concerned 'the political institutions relating to commerce, to finances, to the ecclesiastical and military establishments'.[48] These last two parts, for which students' lecture notes were discovered in 1895, 1958 and 1970, can be discerned as the framework supporting *The Wealth of Nations*.

As a lecturer, Smith was held not to possess quite the eloquence of his master, Hutcheson, but dull he was not. Millar's reminiscence is a study in intellectual exhilaration. Millar told Dugald Stewart:

> He often appeared, at first, not to be sufficiently possessed of the subject, and spoke with some hesitation. As he advanced, however, the matter seemed to crowd upon him, his manner became warm and animated, and his expression easy and fluent. In points susceptible of controversy, you could easily discern that he secretly conceived an opposition to his opinions, and that he was led upon this account to support them with greater energy and vehemence. By the fulness and variety of his illustrations, the subject gradually swelled in his hands, and acquired a dimension which, without a tedious repetition of the same views, was calculated to seize the attention of his audience, and to afford them pleasure, as well as instruction, in following the same object, through all the diversity of shades and aspects in which it was presented, and afterwards in tracing it backwards to that original proposition or general truth from which this beautiful train of speculation had proceeded.

According to Rae, stucco busts of Smith appeared in the booksellers' windows.[49]

James Boswell, the inventor of modern biography with his *Life* of Dr Johnson, attended both of Smith's classes, moral philosophy and rhetoric. He was captivated by a remark of Smith's that even the smallest detail is of interest in a great man, such as that the poet John Milton wore laces rather than buckles in his shoes.[50] Always prone to depression himself, Boswell found his professor also suffered from low spirits, when he would murmur, 'a day in bed – a day in bed'.[51]

Smith's reputation attracted aristocratic pupils, both English and Scottish, including Henry Herbert, later Lord Porchester; David Steuart Erskine, later Lord Buchan; and Thomas Petty Fitzmaurice, son of the first Earl of Shelburne and younger brother of the second Earl, who, as Prime Minister, was to concede independence to the Americans. Smith's letters to Shelburne describe a regime for the seventeen-year-old Thomas that was little short of punishing. The boy had no leisure now for the 'very violent' exercise he had enjoyed at Eton, Smith reported. Two hours with Smith, and an hour each with the professors of logic, Greek, mathematics and Latin, 'makes his hours which he attends every day except Saturday and Sunday to be six in all'. After term came down, Thomas was set to French, dancing and fencing, some Euclid, and three hours of philosophy with Smith himself, 'so that he will not be idle in the vacation'. Lectured by Shelburne on the virtues of 'oeconomy' even for those of large fortune, Smith kept Thomas on a guinea a month pocket-money, after he had squandered four on prints and baubles and 'upon nuts, apples and oranges'.[52] When Thomas fell into a fever, Smith had two doctors in attendance – one, the great Joseph Black – and the letters he wrote to Shelburne during the illness are models of solicitude. When Shelburne grumbled about distractions from the success of the *Theory*, Smith wrote: 'I can ... assure Your Lordship that I have come under no engagements which I look upon as so sacred as those by which I am bound as a member of this University to do everything in my power to serve the young people who are sent here to study.'[53]

Though living in Glasgow, Smith took part in the projects of his Edinburgh friends. The Edinburgh–Glasgow stagecoach brought him into town in time for early-afternoon dinner. He was elected in 1752 to the Philosophical Society, and two years later was a founder member and first chairman of the Select Society, formed on the principle of town Academies in France and Italy to promote both learning and industry.

It was a tense time in Edinburgh. In the absence of a parliament, political conflicts were played out in the General Assembly of the Church of Scotland. This was then divided between a fierce, democratic party attached to the enthusiasm of the seventeeth century, and a more polite and aristocratic party, generally known as the Moderates, that wished to take Scots religion out of the tented meeting and into the drawing-room and had no qualms about associating with men of suspect religion such as Henry Home, now elevated to Scotland's highest court as Lord Kames, and Hume.

At the Assembly of 1755, the High-flyers pounced, seeking a motion to excommunicate both men. The attempt foundered, in part, as Smith thought, because of the charm and beauty of David Hume's personality.[54] The Select Society was a defensive measure to bring together the progressive elements in the Church, the Law and small nobility to entrench a lay civilisation in Scotland. The dispute then moved to a new battleground, which was the theatre, where the Revd John Home's *Tragedy of Douglas* played to packed houses in December

1756. Movements of censure against Home and Alexander Carlyle were a failure and under the historian William Robertson, who was also principal of the University, the Moderates dominated the General Assembly until the 1780s.

For all his tepid religion, Smith much admired the parsimony and independence of the Presbyterian clergy, both in Scotland and, later, in Geneva. 'There is scarce perhaps to be found anywhere in Europe a more learned, decent, independent and respectable set of men,' he wrote in *The Wealth of Nations*.[55] From the *Douglas* affair, he drew the conclusion that the state should give 'entire liberty' to diversions such as painting, music, dancing and the theatre 'to dissipate ... that melancholy and gloomy humour which is almost always the nurse of popular superstition and enthusiasm'.[56] He seems to have been less liberal when it came to young people. Back in Glasgow, he served on a college committee in the winter of 1762–3 set up to lobby the town council against the opening of a playhouse in the town.[57]

The progressive ministers and lawyers launched a journal, the short-lived *Edinburgh Review* of 1755–6. Neither Hume nor Kames took part, but Smith wrote for both of the only two issues published and once again we see in Smith prudence preceding loyalty. In the first issue, of August 1755, he criticised Dr Johnson's dictionary – as insufficiently 'grammatical' or, as we'd say, analytical – in an article which may or may not have been the foundation of their vigorous and lasting enmity.[58] Unpractically, Smith devotes two full pages to the particle 'but'.

In the second number, which appeared in March 1756, Smith showed he was abreast of new thought in France, including the *Encyclopédie*, edited by Denis Diderot and the mathematician Jean le Rond d'Alembert, L. J. Levesque de Pouilly's psychology of pleasure, *Théorie des sentimens agréables*, and Rousseau's *Discours sur les fondemens de l'inégalité parmi les hommes*, presented to the Academy at Dijon and printed in 1755. Levesque de Pouilly's brilliant and influential little book, which was a kind of French answer to Hutcheson and Shaftesbury, gave Smith the title *The Theory of Moral Sentiments*. Rousseau's romance of the 'savage state' captivated Europe and America and survives as a sort of phantom in both Smith's large philosophical works: in the admiration for the native North American and West African in the *Theory of Moral Sentiments* and the pursuit of 'perfect liberty' in *The Wealth of Nations*. Smith translated three long sections of Rousseau's essay, including one beautiful sentence that might have stood epigraph to the *Theory*: 'The savage lives in himself, the man of society always out of himself.'[59] Smith ends his review with a mischievous paean to the 'Republic of Geneva'. As he grew older, Smith grew more and more republican. In the revisions to the *Theory* printed in 1789, he warns that of all political reformers the most dangerous are 'sovereign princes'.[60]

The 'Forty-five had buried Edinburgh's dream of a romantic independence under French protection. The question was how to adjust to the new commercial modernity coming north from England. Hutcheson, both in the *Short Introduction to Moral Philosophy* of 1747 and especially in Book Two of the posthumous *System of Moral Philosophy* of 1755, had discussed value and price, money and interest, with such enthusiasm as almost to forget the jurisprudential framework of his argument. In the *Treatise*, Hume had described the 'partition of employments', or what Smith was to call the division of labour, as one of the attractions of society to human beings and sources of their notions of justice. In his *Political Discourses* of 1752, Hume included seven essays on commercial themes in which he demolished the prejudices of a hundred years. The prosperity of other nations – even France – was of benefit, not detrimental, to Britain, there was no inherent conflict between trade and agriculture, the precious metals were merely mediums of exchange. 'The Political Discourses of Mr Hume,' said Dugald Stewart, 'were evidently of greater use to Mr Smith, than any other book that had appeared prior to his lectures.'[61]

Smith's own interest in commercial questions must be reconstructed from hints in Stewart's eulogy. Smith told Stewart that he had lectured on trade and industry in Edinburgh and then again in Glagow in the winter of 1751–2. In 1755, according to Stewart, anxious to the point of panic that his ideas might be appropriated, Smith had delivered a paper in public that enumerated 'certain leading principles, both political and literary, to which he was anxious to establish his exclusive right.' Who the plagiarist was, or who they were, Stewart was too tactful to say. He was, after all, speaking at the Royal Society of Edinburgh and did not wish 'to revive the memory of private differences'. Adam Ferguson and William Robertson spring to mind.

Smith's paper has not turned up but Stewart's quotations show that *The Wealth of Nations* was not only in embryo, but in a more radical form than we now possess. 'Little else is requisite,' Stewart quotes the paper as as saying, 'to carry a state to the highest degree of opulence from the lowest barbarism, but peace, easy taxes, and a tolerable administration of justice.' Nature could then take its course. 'All governments which thwart this natural course, which force things into another channel, or which endeavour to arrest the progress of society at a particular point, are unnatural, and to support themselves are obliged to be oppressive and tyrannical.'[62] There is nothing so aggressively naturalistic in the version of *The Wealth of Nations* that was published in 1776.

In 1755, the Select Society founded a subsidiary, 'The Edinburgh Society for encouraging arts, sciences, manufactures, and agriculture in Scotland', which was to meet on the first Monday of each month, and award premiums, 'partly honorary, partly lucrative', for Scottish enterprise. Hume wrote in enthusiasm to the painter Allan Ramsay that in the high preoccupations of the Select 'we have not neglected porter, strong ale, and wrought ruffles, even down to linen rags.'[63] Hume was optimist enough to believe, as he wrote in 'Of Refinement in the Arts' (1752), that 'the same age, which produces great philosophers and politicians, renowned generals and poets, usually abounds with skilful weavers and ship-carpenters.'[64] (Ramsay disliked this plebeian or banausic trend and withdrew from the Select Society for fame in London.) With the outbreak of war with France in 1756, new questions arose. Was Britain weakened as a military power by its commercial character? Could the war be paid for by borrowing from the public? Should the colonies be responsible for their own defence?

Smith never shone in the Edinburgh clubs. Alexander Carlyle, one of a new breed of smart Moderate churchmen who later came to envy Smith's aristocratic friendships, said he heard the philosopher speak 'but once', when he opened the inaugural meeting of the Select in May 1754. Otherwise, Smith seems to have passed his social hours sunk out of sight in his mental compositions.

'He was the most absent man in company that I ever saw,' Carlyle continued. 'Moving his lips and talking to himself, and smiling, in the midst of large companys. If you awak'd him from his reverie, and made him attend to the subject of conversation, he immediatly began a harangue and never stop'd till he told you all he knew about it, with the utmost philosophical ingenuity. He knew nothing of characters.'[65]

3

Pen-knives and Snuff-boxes

1759

*T*he *Theory of Moral Sentiments*, when it appeared with the publisher Andrew Millar in London in April 1759, showed what Smith was up to in his Scottish reveries. Never was there a more fascinated inspector of his own sensations or the customs and manners of a society learning to be civilised.

The Theory of Moral Sentiments is the culmination and swansong of a long British tradition of moral questioning that goes back through Hume and Hutcheson, Mandeville, Shaftesbury, Locke and Hobbes into the political and religious ferment of the civil wars of the seventeenth century. Finished with popes, priests and absolute princes, the British wanted to find their own way to what was right and what was wrong.

Yet with its pen-knives and snuff-boxes, tweezer-cases, ear-pickers, nail-cutters, chests of drawers and haunch buttons, its bad roads and clumsy servants, its jokes fallen flat and its aldermen's wives jostling one another for the best seat at table,[1] the *Theory* extends the inquiry into the territory of fashion and manners, or what Thomas Hobbes called 'small morals'. An exquisite distinction of feeling and precise gradation of generous or selfish sentiment are incorporated into moral types – The Proud Man, The Vain Man, The Foolish Liar, The Important Coxcomb, The Man For Whom Absolutely Nothing At All Is Right[2] – that have one foot in Aristotle and Theophrastus and the other in Oliver Goldsmith's *The Vicar of Wakefield*. Henceforth, the chief territory for moralising will be not the sermon or the philosophical tract but the dressing-table novel.

Those who believe philosophy should confine itself to universals – water, not the River Tweed; music, not Handel – will find *The Theory of Moral Sentiments* an odd sort of philosophy. But it entranced a British and continental public caught up in a cult of sensibility and virtue. 'They who live thus in a great city,' Smith had predicted in a lecture, 'where they have the free liberty of disposing of their wealth in all the luxuries and refinements of life; who are not called to any publick employment but what they inclined to – naturally turn their attention to the motions of the human mind, and those events that were accounted for by the different internall affections that influenced the persons concerned, would be what most suited their taste.'

In short, 'Sentiment must bee what will chiefly interest such a people.'[3]

Hume, whose own philosophical masterpiece had failed back in 1739, rose on 12 April to that most gruelling challenge for the philosopher, the success of his friend. He took refuge in facetiousness. 'Three bishops calld yesterday at Millar's shop [in the Strand in London] in order to buy copies, and to ask questions about the author: The Bishop of Peterborough said he had passd the evening in a company, where he heard it extolld above all books in the world. You may conclude what opinion true philosophers will entertain of it, when these retainers to superstition praise it so highly ... Millar exults and brags that two thirds of the edition are already sold, and that he is now sure of success.'[4]

Edmund Burke, whose sentimental aesthetics *On the Sublime and Beautiful* had been the philosophical sensation of two summers earlier, raved about Smith in the *Annual Register*: 'One of the most beautiful fabrics of moral theory, that has ever appeared ... A new, and at the same time a perfectly natural road of speculation ... Rather painting than writing.'[5] In a private letter of congratulation on 10 September, he wrote: 'a theory like yours founded on the Nature of man, which is always the same, will last, when those that are founded on his opinions, which are always changing, will and must be forgotten.'[6] The *Theory* ran through six English editions in Smith's lifetime, was translated into French and German, and was not eclipsed by *The Wealth of Nations* till the rise of political economy amid the battles and factory smoke of the Victorian age.

The title is an exact bill of philosophical goods. *The Theory of Moral Sentiments* seeks to explain not why such an action is right and such an action is wrong, but how, in a world that has dispensed with external authority, *how we come to feel they are so.* It is a search not for a doctrine of what is right and good for human beings at all times but for a theory of how human beings form judgements of what is right and wrong on particular occasions. We learn not why women should be chaste, but why men feel they should be so. (It is only in the last book of the *Theory* that Smith poses the classic question of the moralist, 'Wherein does virtue consist?'[7] The answer, after a summary, even, with respect, slapdash survey of philosophical moralities ancient and modern, is more or less the Stoical notion of prudence.)

Ralph Cudworth and Samuel Clarke had argued that it was the reasoning mind that distinguished between right and wrong. The London and Paris wits, and particularly Mandeville, pronounced that right was merely reasonable self-interest. Hutcheson retorted that not reason but a sort of super-sensation caused humanity to derive pleasure from the perception of good actions, and pain from bad. He called this faculty Moral Sense. Hume thought the 'chief source of moral distinctions'[8] was sympathy, and his friend agreed.

Smith opens the book with a bow to the shades of Hobbes and Mandeville, then summons his beloved teacher Hutcheson to speak: 'How selfish soever man may be supposed, there are evidently some principles in his nature, which interest him in the fortune of others, and render their happiness necessary to him.'[9]

It had long been assumed that we examine the morality of our own actions, and then use the results of that self-examination to judge the actions of others. Adam Smith's first innovation was to turn that on its head. He said that we judge first of the morality of others, and then come back to judge ourselves. We put ourselves in their position, and by means of *sympathy* or *fellow-feeling* which is the principle or pivot of Smith's system, we seek to experience – even for just a moment and in however faint a reflection – the sensations that gave rise to their actions.

It is through sympathy that we imagine the happiness of the rich and successful, follow the fashions they set, pursue ambition beyond our animal requirements and submit to distinctions of social class. It is by the degree of congruence with our own sensations that we judge the rightness, or as Smith calls it the *propriety*, of the actions and opinions of other people.

In transferring those sympathetic judgements to ourselves, by means of a combination of experience and rules to which Smith gives the name and character of an Impartial Spectator, we acquire our sense of right conduct or duty. In other words, we acquire from other people our notions of ourselves as moral actors and actresses. If this is Christianity, it is Christianity turned inside out: 'As to love our neighbour as we love ourselves is the great law of Christianity,' Smith writes, 'so it is the great precept of nature to love ourselves only as we love our neighbour.'[10]

'And the soul,' said Plato, 'if it is to know itself, must look into a soul.'[11] 'As we have no immediate experience of what other men feel,' Smith writes at the opening of the *Theory*, 'we can form no idea of the manner in which they are affected, but by conceiving what we ourselves should feel in a like situation.'[12] This sympathy is not, he states, only pity and compassion but 'may now ... be made use of to denote our fellow-feeling with any passion whatever'.[13] Sympathy is spontaneous, even spasmodic, as when 'the mob, when they are gazing at a dancer on the slack-rope, naturally writhe and twist and balance their own bodies, as they see him do, and as they feel that they themselves must do if in his situation.'[14]

This sympathy is carried from the circus or raree-show into the moral arena. When we judge another's action, we do not simply look at its outcome (as Hume had argued). We do not consider (to give a modern example) someone who gambles on the lottery meritorious, just because a fraction of his or her outlay will go towards building a museum. We are concerned with the motive or propriety of actions, and we judge of the propriety of others only by their coincidence with that which we feel when we put ourselves in the same circumstances. If we are in sympathy with their emotions or passions, we judge them proper. If not, not.

From those premises, Smith conjures an array of social phenomena that are both interesting in themselves and useful to the good order and lustre of society. For sympathy to function as a social mechanism, emotions must be calibrated. The spectator attempts as much as possible to raise the pitch of his sympathetic emotion, while the person displaying emotion attempts to restrain it to the level of the spectator. Both strive to reach what Smith called, in one of those oxymorons he loved, a 'pitch of moderation',[15] from which all manner of social virtues instantly appear: on the part of the sympathiser, attentiveness and humanity, on the part of the sympathised, self-government and self-control.

We approve of displays of emotion only in so far as we can sympathise with them. Shrieks of pain or fright are unbecoming because the spectator cannot hope to match in sympathy the agony or terror felt by the sufferer. Displays of sexual partiality are particularly hard to sympathise with. There is a 'grossness … which mixes with, and is, perhaps, the foundation of love' which is offensive at close quarters.[16] Sexual love always appear to outsiders 'entirely disproportioned to the value of its object', and all expressions of love made to a third person, unless self-deprecating, are ridiculous.[17]

Smith goes on to argue that we sympathise more strongly with displays of social or benevolent emotions than with shows of resentment or hatred, mere bursts of egotistical joy or sorrow, or that endless small discontent that is so wearisome to the observer. Here is an example of how Smith builds a psychological type through an accretion of narrative detail, in the manner of *The Spectator* and La Bruyère and beyond them the antique master of ethical character, Theophrastus:

The man who is made uneasy by every little disagreeable incident, who is hurt if either the cook or the butler have failed in the least article of their duty, who feels every defect in the highest ceremonial of politeness, whether it be shewn to himself or to any other person, who takes it amiss that his intimate friend did not bid him good-morrow when they met in the forenoon, and that his brother hummed a tune all the time he himself was telling a story; who is put out of humour by the badness of the weather when in the country, by the badness of the roads when upon a journey, and by the want of company, and dulness of all public diversions when in town; such a person, I say, though he should have some reason, will seldom meet with much sympathy.[18]

Smith is an important link between the ancient conception of character (for rhetorical or ethical purpose) and the 'character' as actor or actress in a novel.

Having established the psychology of moral judgement, Smith then proposes to show how it operates. In every case, he says, we tend to look more to the motive in each action than to its outcome and to concern ourselves more with its *propriety* than its *merit*. As for the propriety of our feelings and the merit of our actions, we invoke the judgement not of conscience (which smacks of the Sunday School) but of society itself. Aware of what our society thinks, we become spectators of our own appearance and behaviour, and make our judgements of both.

It is worth remembering that, in poor old Scotland, the generation of Hume and Smith was the first to inhabit rooms hung with looking-glasses, and some of the novelty of mirrors still glitters in their reasoning. Hume wrote of sympathy flashing back and forth between persons, as if mirrors had been set to face each other. For Smith, society is 'the only looking-glass by which we can, in some measure, with the eyes of other people, scrutinize the propriety of our own conduct'.[19] After all, as he wrote in the 'Imitative Arts', 'One's own face becomes then the most agreeable object which a looking-glass can represent to us, and the only object which we do not soon grow weary with looking at.'[20]

But the mirror of society is dark or distorted. On almost all matters of importance to us, we find our friends, family and neighbours ill-informed, partial and prejudiced. In one more ingenious twist to the argument, Smith tells us we submit not only to the actual judgement of our peers but to a higher instance, 'the supposed impartial and well-informed spectator, to that of a man within the breast'.[21] This 'man within', a collection of general rules about what is to be done and what to be avoided, is a sort of ideal balance to worldly misjudgement and our own self-delusion; or as Burns had it, 'O wad some Pow'r the giftie gie us / To see oursels as ithers see us!', as he stared at the louse on a pretty girl's bonnet in Mauchline church. Propriety or rightness is therefore marked by the 'degree of any passion which the impartial spectator approves of'.[22]

The beauty of the *Theory* lies in its ingenuity, its democratic and anti-authoritarian character and its optimism. It is easier to believe that we draw our notion of ourselves, and of right, from others rather than from a Moral Sense which, as Smith said, had waited a long time to be invented.[23] The minute anatomy of emotions in isolation will seem a little old-fashioned in the age of the subconscious. But society itself appears in entirely modern guise as a sort of immense network of stimulation and reaction that needs neither direction from above nor maintenance from below.

The fault of the *Theory* is a certain stateliness, in which morality vanishes behind good breeding. Scotland had only just dispensed with the fire-and-brimstone field-meeting, the bottle and the dagger. The Greeks Smith admired had taught that wisdom was the avoidance of excess in all things. The violent emotions, which were to fascinate the two generations after Smith, are toned down or, in the case of sexual passion, ignored.

From his attachment to his mother, and his admiration for the ancient world, it was not to be expected that Smith, any more than Plato, should be given to gallantry. The cult of women that followed on, as it were naturally, on the disarming and domestication of Scottish life in the eighteenth century quite passed him by. There is nothing of Hutcheson's high-minded rapture at the ethical value of sexual love, or Ferguson's paean to medieval chivalry, or John Millar's great political history of sex or Burns's libertine metaphysics.[24]

Women for Smith were not capable of humanity, but only of that 'exquisite fellow-feeling' that requires no self-denial or self-control or exertion.[25] As for the feelings between the sexes, love was natural, and appropriate to a certain age of life, but also 'a weakness', which the Spartans and American Indians regarded as an 'unpardonable effeminacy' or 'sordid necessity'.[26] Yet Smith's ignorance of women seems less the misogyny of Plato then the prudery of the Islamic philosophers. The pioneer feminist Mary Wollstonecraft, in *A Vindication of the Rights of Woman* published in the turbulent 1790s, greatly admired the *Theory* and simply feminised one of Smith's characters, the Young Nobleman, into the modern 'lady'.[27]

In the first edition, Smith seems to have given the impression to some readers that the Impartial Spectator was mere established social attitudes (which, of course, are established for reasons other than their moral precision). In a letter to Smith that can be reconstructed from the philosopher's reply, Sir Gilbert Elliot, a friend of Hume and MP for Selkirk, must have made precisely that point. Put in today's language, if the Impartial Spectator is a reflection of social attitudes, how is he any more worthy of our attention than the pub bore, the ranting newspaper column, the conversation on the bus, the paranoid Friday sermon, the hectoring talk-radio host? In his reply to Elliot, and in the first revisions, Smith retorted that imagination can conjure a spectator free of ignorance and prejudice in the same way that the imagination corrects our perceptions of a landscape, turning those lawns and woods and arms of the sea that fill a study window from small to large, and from two into three dimensions.[28] 'Real magnanimity and conscious virtue,' he told Elliot, 'can support itselfe under the disapprobation of mankind.'[29]

Smith tinkered with the Impartial Spectator in later editions without in any way resolving the problem. In the last consistent piece of thinking he did in his life, the revisions to the sixth edition done in 1789, Smith made an important distinction: while the public judges on praise, the Impartial Spectator judges on praiseworthiness.

'The jurisdiction of the man without,' he wrote, 'is founded altogether in the desire of actual praise, and in the aversion to actual blame. The jurisdiction of the man within, is founded altogether in the desire of praise-worthiness, and in the aversion to blame-worthiness; in the desire of possessing those qualities, and performing those actions, which we love and admire in other people; and in the dread of possessing those qualities, and performing those actions, which we hate and despise in other people.'[30]

The Impartial Spectator or man within becomes more experienced and more trustworthy by the constant observation of character and conduct, and by practice. 'It is the slow, gradual, and progressive work of the great demigod within the breast, the great judge and arbiter of conduct ... Every day some feature is improved; every day some blemish is corrected ... He endeavours, as well as he can, to assimilate his own character to this archetype of perfection.'[31] In other words, there are standards of right and wrong quite a bit more refined than the sympathy for and of our fellows and we are, as it were, back to square one.

Meanwhile, in replacing divine law with human arrangements, and schemes of dogmatic morality with imaginary social judgement, Smith leaves society prey to manipulation. He himself warned of the effect on morality of custom in, say, the practice of exposing unwanted children in China and ancient Greece, or, at a less ghastly level, sending them off to boarding school or on the Grand Tour.[32]

Smith was always uneasy about a society that is forever gaping at the rich and fortunate at the expense of the wise and the kind. In a section that might have made a sentimental novella, Smith writes of a poor man's son, 'whom heaven in its anger has visited with ambition'.[33] The boy pursues riches that are merely 'enormous and operose machines to produce a few trifling conveniences ... immense fabrics, which it requires the labour of a life to raise, which threaten every moment to overwhelm the person that dwells in them'.[34]

The way out for Smith is not moral but political. Riches are a mere 'deception' but their pursuit keeps in motion the industry of mankind.[35] Respect for wealth and high birth helps establish social class and maintain the subordination of society.[36] Anway, it is easier for the 'great mob of mankind' to descry riches and high birth than the 'invisible and often uncertain difference of virtue'.[37] Communities can be held together not by affection or obligation, but by 'a mercenary exchange of good offices according to an agreed valuation'.[38]

Mouldering in continental exile, the Jacobite philosopher Sir James Steuart recognised that there was something new and different about commercial society. 'Modern luxury is *systematical*,' he was writing. 'It cannot make one step, but at the expence of an adequate equivalent, acquired by those who stand most in need of the protection and assistance of their fellow citizens; and without producing a vibration [alteration] in the balance of their wealth.'[39] In France, the Marquis de Mirabeau (father of the revolutionary orator) pronounced: 'The whole magic of a well-ordered society is that each man works for others, while believing that he is working for himself.'[40]

Smith anticipated them. The rich follow their own footling lives, but are obliged by the very operation of money and free commerce to share some of their riches with the poor.

> The rich only select from the heap what is most precious and agreeable. They consume little more than the poor, and in spite of their natural selfishness and rapacity, though they mean only their own conveniency, though the sole end which they propose from the labours of all the thousands whom they employ, be the gratification of their own vain and insatiable desires, they divide with the poor the produce of all their improvements.

That sounds fair enough, but then Smith goes on:

> They are led by an invisible hand to make nearly the same distribution of the necessaries of life, which would have been made, had the earth been divided into equal portions among all its inhabitants.[41]

Here, at its second public appearance, the Invisible Hand has gone through an alteration. By 1759, the theological orthodoxy of the early eighteenth century in Scotland had abated. Yet Smith was still a professor engaged in instructing young men destined for the cloth. Though he had little time for scripture, Smith was not inclined entirely to dispense with theological final causes. The Invisible Hand here is like the Great Superintendant, or Superintendant of the Universe, or Great Conductor or Benevolent Nature and all the other deistic codewords that litter the *Theory*.[42] In the next sentence, Smith adds a helpful gloss. 'When Providence divided the earth among a few lordly masters, it neither forgot nor abandoned those who seemed to have been left out of the partition. These last too enjoy their share of all that it produces.'

That is optimism run wild. A visitor to the 1750s Highlands or a modern *favela* would not consider that the 'necessaries of life' had been divided into nearly equal portions. Smith rescues his argument by a small tactical retreat. 'In what constitutes the real happiness of human life, they are in no respect inferior to those who would seem so much above them.' This real happiness, it turns out, is the freedom from worldly care of the ancient Stoics. There follows one of those sentences where the reader seems actually to be at Smith's side, and everything is forgiven. 'In ease of body and peace of mind, all the different ranks of life are nearly upon a level, and the beggar who suns himself by the side of the highway, possesses the same security which kings are fighting for.'[43]

4

Infidel with a Bag Wig

1759–1776

Smith ended *The Theory of Moral Sentiments* with a promise that he could not keep but never disavowed. Passing on from virtue to what he called a very exact form of virtue – namely, justice – he proposed in the last paragraph to offer his readers a philosophy of natural justice, or what he called a 'those principles which ought to run through and be the foundation of the laws of all nations'.

The problem was that those principles were hard to disentangle from the actual systems of law and government obtaining in the world, which had been warped by government or 'the interest of particular orders of men who tyrannise the government' or wrong-headed judicial custom or plain barbarism. Smith was promising nothing less than a philosophical examination of the *ancien régime* in Europe and its colonies: 'an account of the general principles of law and government, and of the different revolutions they have undergone in the different ages and periods of society, not only in what concerns justice, but in what concerns police, revenue, and arms, and whatever else is the object of law.'[1]

This work was, after the doomed philosophy of the arts and sciences already mentioned, the second of the great unfinished projects of Smith's life. How important it was to Smith is clear from an advertisement he added to the sixth edition of the *Theory*, published in the year of his death. The part of the promise relating to police, revenue and arms, Smith had in *The Wealth of Nations* 'partly executed'. (By *police* Smith did not mean the constabulary. It was a French term devised to cover such workaday government responsibilities as street-cleaning and street-lighting, fire prevention, and regulating and supervising food and other basic supplies. A *lieutenant-général de police de la ville de Paris* was first appointed in 1677.)

What remained was the system of 'natural justice', to which Smith addresses himself in a tone of regret. In style, and particularly that *sympathetic* conveyance of sentiment that he spoke of in the lectures on rhetoric,[2] these are the most affecting sentences Smith ever wrote. 'My very advanced age leaves me, I acknowledge, very little expectation of ever being able to execute this great work to my own satisfaction; yet, as I have not altogether abandoned the design, and as I wish still to continue under the obligation of doing what I can, I have allowed the paragraph to remain as it was published more than thirty years ago, when I entertained no doubt of being able to execute every thing which it announced.'[3]

Notes towards this project – contained in some or even all of 'eighteen thin paper folio books'[4] – Smith ordered to be burned unread. Yet this phantom work has come to fascinate scholars in Britain and North America. It is as if they were searching for philosophy to repair some of the moral deficiencies of modern political economy. Can we return to inquire at Smith's tomb and summon this revolutionary apparition from the damps of the Edinburgh Canongate?

The answer is 'No'. What we have is *The Wealth of Nations*, and three sets of students' notes from Smith's class on the philosophy of law or jurisprudence in the 1760s. One set, published by Edwin Cannan in 1896, is dated '1766' but seems to be a fair copy made by a professional copyist of the lectures of 1763–4.[5] In those days before textbooks, it was common practice so to duplicate lectures by a popular professor. The second set, found by John M. Lothian at a country-house auction in Aberdeen in 1958, appears to be a verbatim report written up from shorthand notes during the course of lectures of the previous winter. While the material is similar, the organisation is not. The 1762–3 course begins with property and inheritance and family law and then goes on to government and police; the later course begins with government. The police sections cover topics such as the division of labour, money and prices as Hutcheson had done in his lectures back in the 1730s. A third set, written by Smith's Glasgow colleague John Anderson in his commonplace book (now at the college he founded, the University of Strathclyde), consists of partial notes of the jurisprudence lectures one year in the 1750s.[6] It was published by R. L. Meek in 1976.

What is the pivot of Smith's system of jurisprudence, presuming that it ever had one?

It appears to have been the Impartial Spectator. In other words, in the early 1760s, Smith was still of the belief that the core elements of the *Theory* – sympathy and moral observation – might yet prove the basis of a reforming political philosophy. In what seems to be notes to or a fragment of his lectures on ethics, now printed as an appendix to the *Theory of Moral Sentiments*, he talks of giving a separate discussion or 'particular discourse' on the moral background to the mixture of statute, custom, common law and equity that makes up a system of civil and criminal justice: in Smith's words, 'the rules by which it [i.e. an existing system of justice] is most suitable to the natural principles of Justice, or to the Analogy of those Sentiments upon which our Sense of it is founded that such decisions should be regulated.'[7] In the later Glasgow jurisprudence lectures, Smith invokes sympathy and the Impartial (or Indifferent) Spectator as a basis for judgements of the rightness of ownership or possession, and for the severity of punishments.[8]

Yet Smith runs into a dilemma which he dramatises by the example of a sentry, who is executed for having slept on watch. What could be more just than that one man be sacrificed to the security of thousands, though 'in our hearts we would be glad to save' him?[9] At this distance, it is hard to see how the Impartial Spectator could provide a set of precise and exact laws holding across all circumstances and societies. The Spectator's mimosa-like sensitivity to social context has little place in jurisprudence. Perhaps, too, Smith was reluctant to launch such a frontal assault on the systems of power and privilege in eighteenth-century European society. In *The Wealth of Nations*, Smith prefers to talk first about the utility or expediency of this or that policy, and only later of its justice. 'It is but equity, besides ...', he writes, without explaining how such judgements of equity are reached. All this will be a disappointment to readers from the political Left. Others will give Smith the credit for knowing what he could and couldn't do.

That still left the complex of police, revenue and arms. Already by the early 1760s, Smith was seeking to organise his ideas on those topics into a coherent survey. Three manuscripts composed by Smith have survived, and appear to come from this period. The most extensive was found by W. R. Scott in papers that had belonged to the English statesman Charles Townshend. 'An Early Draft of Part of *The Wealth of Nations*', as Scott called it, exhibits some striking correspondences with the printed version. It consists of a chapter of thirty-one connected pages on the division of labour, along with summaries of three more chapters dealing with price and exchange; money; and impediments, natural and political, to what the writer calls the 'Progress of Opulence'. According to W. R. Scott, it was dictated to a Glasgow University scribe.[10] Amid other evidence, an innocent reference to Ossian, the mythical Scottish bard, dates the manuscript to the early 1760s: that is, after the sensational appearance of James MacPherson's *Fragments of Ancient Poetry Collected in the Highlands of Scotland and Translated from the Galic or Erse Language* in 1760 and before the English attack on their authenticity gained volume and venom in the second half of 1763. The two other fragments, found by Scott in papers that had come down from Smith's heir, David Douglas, cover aspects of the division of labour.[11]

In his letter of congratulation on *The Theory of Moral Sentiments* in September 1759, Hume had added a piece of news: 'Charles Townshend, who passes for the cleverest fellow in England, is so taken with the performance, that he said to Oswald [of Dunnikier] he wou'd put the Duke of Buccleugh under the authors care, and woud endeavour to make it worth his while to accept of that charge.'[12]

Charles Townshend flashed like a comet across the political firmament. Born in 1725, the scion of improving Norfolk agriculturists, he entered parliament in his family's interest at the age of twenty-one. As Chancellor of the Exchequer under a weak Prime Minister, Townshend attempted in early 1767 to raise revenue in America by imposing tea and other duties and establishing commissioners of customs at the colonial ports of Boston, New York, Philadelphia, Baltimore and Savannah. Then, having set his American time-bomb, he died of a fever that September, at the age of forty-two.

But in the spring of 1759, he was lately married to the widowed Lady Dalkeith, and become stepfather to her three young children, including the twelve-year-old Henry Scott, third Duke of Buccleuch. That summer, Townshend came up to Scotland hoping to use his wife's family influence to pursue his political career, but fell foul of the entrenched power of his wife's cousin, the Duke of Argyll.

Townshend visited Edinburgh, attended the Select Society where he complained about the Scots accent, and visited Smith in Glasgow. The obituary of Smith that appeared in *The Times* of 24 July 1790 related how, while taking Townshend round the Glasgow manufactures, Smith was so engaged in the division of labour that he fell into a tanners' pit. In a letter to Townshend of 17 September, Smith says nothing of tanners' pits or the division of labour, but does speak of some books Townshend had ordered from the university press for the young Duke to have with him at Eton College.[13] The list includes the beautiful Foulis folio Homer, the Greek tragedians and historians, Smith's beloved Stoic philosophers Epictetus and Marcus Aurelius, and the *Characters* of Theophrastus.[14]

On 25 October 1763, Townshend wrote to say that the Duke would be leaving Eton at Christmas and to ask if Smith were still disposed to travel abroad with him.[15]

Now Smith disapproved of the temptations of the Grand Tour, as worse even than the English boarding schools and universities. The only advantage, he wrote in *The Wealth of Nations*, was that 'by sending his son abroad, a father delivers himself, at least for some time, from so disagreeable an object as a son unemployed, neglected, and going to ruin before his eyes.'[16] Hume, for one, had thought in 1759 that Smith would never abandon his professorship for such a jaunt.[17]

Much had happened since then. Smith's horizons had receded. The *Theory* had been a European success. Beset in the spring of 1760 by one of his mysterious illnesses, Smith had been ordered by Dr Cullen to ride five hundred miles before the summer was out. (He planned to ride down as far as Yorkshire and come back up the west side of England.) The following year he made his first visit to London in the company, according to Rae, of the future Prime Minister, Lord Shelburne, elder brother of his old pupil Thomas Fitzmaurice.[18]

The Seven Years War, which had embargoed travel to the Continent, had ended with the Peace of Paris in April 1763. Hume, who came to Paris that summer as an attaché to the first British Ambassador for seven years, Lord Hertford, had been a brilliant success. Hume's letter of 28 October 1763 from the French court at Fontainebleau is a daze of scent and petticoats, as the fat Scotsman confronted the greatest challenge of all to the philosophical temperament, which is French women. 'Even Mme Pompadour's civilities were, if possible, exceeded by those of the Dutchess of Choiseul,' Hume wrote, and it was some time before he remembered that it was precisely this sort of fine society that had snubbed him when he was struggling to establish himself in Scotland.[19]

Whether investigating his jurisprudence project or police-revenue-arms, Smith needed to study another political society, and why not an absolutist government that stood in a polar relation to the British system of weak king and strong parliament? He was no doubt anxious to meet the French *philosophes* who had received the *Theory* so warmly. In his reply to Hume of 12 December 1763, he asked to be remembered to the Baron d'Holbach and Claude-Adrien Helvétius and 'all the men of genius in France who do me the honour to know anything about me'.[20] He certainly wanted to meet Voltaire, now living at Ferney, near Geneva.

A prudent man turned forty years of age would be bound to consider the terms offered by Townshend: a salary of £300 per year, plus travelling expenses while abroad, and a pension of £300 for life. Punctilious in matters of money, Smith tried to return the annuity once the young Duke had helped establish him as Commissioner of Customs at Edinburgh in 1787, but found the Scott family quite obdurate in its generosity. He was to receive from the Scotts more than £8,000 for three years labour: enough, for example, to fit out two merchantmen for Virginia or build four houses in the fashionable new style in St Andrew's Square in the Edinburgh New Town.[21]

At his farewell lecture in Glasgow, according to the judge Lord

Woodhouselee, Smith tried to return his students their fees for the uncompleted session. Amid a storm of protest, Smith 'seizing by the coat the young man who stood next to him, he thrust the money into his pocket, and then pushed him from him. The rest saw it was in vain to contest the matter, and were obliged to let him take his own way.'[22] That same punctiliousness caused him to resign his chair. In contrast, Adam Ferguson, when he went to England as tutor to Lord Chesterfield, refused to vacate his chair as moral philosophy professor at Edinburgh, and when the Town Council tried to replace him, he took the city to the Court of Session and won.

With Mrs Smith and Janet Douglas secure for at least the year in the house at Professors' Court,[23] Smith left Glasgow in January 1764 to meet the young Duke, who was now seventeen years old. They set out together and arrived in Paris on 13 February. After a few days with Hume in the Faubourg Saint-Germain, they proceeded to their first destination, the city of Toulouse. With its own self-governing *parlement*, academies of art and science and university, Toulouse and its provincial society were thought appropriate to a young Scotsman's education. The town was in the throes of a bitter battle between Voltaire and the forces of religious reaction among the lawyers of the *parlement* who ruled the town on behalf of the King.

Jean Calas, a Protestant cloth merchant, had been accused of strangling his son in his shop on the night of 13 October 1761 to prevent him converting to the Church of Rome. Without the slightest evidence, Calas was condemned to death in a secret trial by the *parlement*. Under torture, he continued to protest his innocence but was *roué* – broken on the wheel and then strangled – on 10 March 1762. Voltaire enlisted all his influence at Court and with the public to force the *parlement,* almost a year later, to reveal its proceedings and justify its sentence. By the time Smith and the young Duke arrived in Toulouse, Catholic feeling in the town was running high but the *parlement* was on the defensive. On 4 June 1764, the Royal Council rejected the proceedings and ordered a retrial. On 12 March 1765, Jean Calas and his family were cleared of wrongdoing and the survivors granted compensation. Jean Calas's indomitable courage under torture left a lifelong impression on Smith. In the final revision to *Theory*, he evoked the sufferings of Jean Calas to illustrate a profound insight: that the victim of injustice may suffer greater remorse than the guilty. 'They are condemned to death and to everlasting infamy. Religion can alone afford them any effectual comfort.'[24]

Townshend had assured Smith that the duc de Choiseul, the King's favourite and Prime Minister, would write letters of recommendation to 'all the people of fashion' in Toulouse and elsewhere. In fact, Smith and Buccleuch knew only a cousin of Hume's who had entered the French Church and gallicised his name, Cuthbert, as the Abbé Seignelay Colbert. Unfortunately, as Smith wrote to Hume on 5 July, Colbert was 'a stranger here almost as much as we'.[25]

Smith never spoke French well[26] and his social inexperience must have been mortifying. What contrast to David Hume at Fontainebleau, where the duchesse de Choiseul had called for him from the other end of the salon. Smith wrote: 'The life which I led at Glasgow was a pleasurable, dissipated life in comparison of that which I lead here at present.' Then he added: 'I have begun to write a book in order to pass away the time.'[27] If, as seems more than probable, Smith had already given or lent the 'Early Draft' to Townshend before leaving Britain, that was an exaggeration. Still, it is pleasant to think of *The Wealth of Nations* as a cure for boredom and loneliness in a French provincial town

For a further diversion, Smith took his charge to the bustling port city of Bordeaux in the late summer. There was a foolish moment when it was found that Lord Hertford's letter of introduction to the Governor of Guienne, Voltaire's able and libertine friend the duc de Richelieu, referred to Smith as Robinson. Hertford must have muddled Smith with Principal William Robertson of Edinburgh, whose *History of Scotland* had appeared at the time of the *Theory* and with equal or greater success.

Yet the trip to Bordeaux went well and Richelieu treated them with the 'utmost politeness and attention'.[28] The party made another jaunt to Bagnères-de-Bigorre, a watering-place in the Pyrenees. As they planned a second to Bordeaux, Smith told Hume on 21 October that the young man was beginning to find his feet in French society, 'and I flatter myself I shall spend the rest of the time we are to live together not only in peace and contentment, but in gayety and amusement.'[29]

At Bordeaux, they picked up Henry's younger brother, Hew. They passed on to Montpellier, for a meeting of the local assembly of the self-governing liberal States of Languedoc, a democratic remnant in the sea of French absolutism. A letter from a Glasgow friend, the tobacco merchant and shipowner John Glassford, on 5 November enquired after 'the usefull work that was so well advanced here'.[30] That, presumably, was *The Wealth of Nations*.

At some point, they made a tour of the south of France before setting out, some time in the autumn of 1765, for Geneva. The city was popular with British tourists for its good order and Protestantism, and for an excellent physician, Théodore Tronchin, who admired Smith so much he had sent his son to Glasgow University in 1761. For Smith there were two other attractions: the city's republican government, and the man he respected as much as anybody living but Hume, François-Marie Arouet, known by his *nom de plume* of Voltaire. Smith liked Voltaire's tragedies *Mahomet* and *L'Orphelin de la Chine*, but he had also read his histories and composed a brilliant character of the Sun King for the *Theory* from the *Siècle de Louis XIV*.[31]

We know nothing of their meetings, for the only letter that survives – and it is almost too good to be true – is from Voltaire's mistress (who was also his niece), Marie-Louise Denis, asking for Smith's help after a party of English sportsmen had trespassed and caused a fracas.[32] Such is and has always been philosophy among the English. In passages added to the *Theory* in later editions, Smith noted Voltaire's extreme sensitivity to criticism – even from Lord Kames, whom he never forgave – and also his impetuousness. It is a passage that sums up not only Smith, but the different styles of 'enlightenment' in Scotland and France.

The prudent man, says Smith, 'respects with an almost religious scrupulosity, all the established decorums and ceremonials of society'. In contrast, men of 'much more splendid talents and virtues', such as Jonathan Swift or Voltaire, 'set the most pernicious example to those who wish to resemble them, and who too often content themselves with imitating their follies, without even attempting to attain their perfections'.[33] For all the republican and anti-clerical tone of *The Wealth of Nations*, Smith was straitlaced in his manners and discreet in his religion and politics.

Smith also met a patient of Dr Tronchin, the duchesse d'Enville, and her son, the young duc de La Rochefoucauld. They became close friends,[34] even though Smith had slighted the boy's famous grandfather in the *Theory*. The offending passage, in which he mentioned the aphorist in the same sentence as Mandeville, Smith excised in the sixth edition.[35] This friendship ensured that when the party at last felt ready to proceed to Paris some time around the turn of 1766, it could expect the *entrée* into a wide circle of philosophical and fashionable acquaintance.

Hume was leaving. Hertford was due to be replaced, and Hume could not make up his mind where he himself should settle: Edinburgh, London, Paris or some sunny provincial town such as Toulouse or Montauban. Smith, who was suffering from homesickness, had had enough of France. 'A man is always displaced in a forreign country,' he wrote. As for the French, 'they live in such large societies, and their affections are dissipated among so great a variety of objects, that they can bestow but a very small share of them upon any individual.' Smith himself was leaning towards London. The anti-Scots feeling in the capital, which was largely directed at the King's Scottish favourite Lord Bute, would dissipate 'in a twelvemonth … Let us make short excursions together sometimes to see our friends in France and sometimes to see our friends in Scotland, but London be the place of our ordinary residence.'[36]

This was mere courtesy. Though fond of each other, each man valued his independence. Apart from a few months in Edinburgh in 1751, a few days in Paris in 1764 and a few weeks in London in 1767, Hume and Smith never lived in the same city. They did not meet this

time, for Hume set out for London on 4 January 1766 in the company
not of Smith but of Jean-Jacques Rousseau, who had been offered
refuge in England from persecution by the Paris *parlement*. 'I am sorry
I did not see you before I left Paris,' Hume wrote from London.[37] (To
the delight of literary Europe, Hume and the paranoiac Rousseau were
soon fighting like dogs.)

The next nine months make a striking interlude in Smith's life.
Though even Hume could not present him as 'a man of the world',[38]
Smith was soon installed with his charges in the Faubourg Saint-
Germain and attending the theatre and the fashionable *salons* of the
capital. The comtesse de Boufflers, the patroness of Rousseau who
back in 1761 had winkled Hume out of the solitudes of Edinburgh,
was kind to him and toyed with the idea of translating the *Theory* into
French. A facetious and enigmatic letter, dated 18 February 1766, and
addressing Smith as '*héros et idole des high-broad* [sic] *Ladys*' asks for
news of the duchesse d'Anville and the comtesse de Boufflers. 'Or is
your heart,' the writer asks, 'still smitten with the charms of Mad. Nicol
or the allure as much open as hidden of that [actually *cetter*] other lady
of Fife?'[39] (Who these women were remains a mystery.[40])

Smith took the two boys to the theatre and the opera, not merely
for diversion but, as Stewart was at pains to point out, to explore 'his
peculiar notions ... with respect to the imitative arts' as part of his philosophical history of the arts and sciences.[41] Two fragments published
after his death, 'Of the Nature of that Imitation which takes place
in what are called The Imitative Arts' and 'On the Affinity between
Music, Dancing and Poetry', must date in part from this period.

Smith became friendly with the former actress and sentimental novelist, Marie-Jeanne Riccoboni. Though Mme Riccoboni disliked his voice and his sticking-out teeth, found him absent-minded and 'ugly as a devil', she adored his sentimental philosophy. Her letter of introduction to the actor David Garrick reveals an unfamiliar Adam Smith. He is *un philosophe, moral et pratique; gay, riant, à cent lieus de la pédanterie des nôtres*'. In short, '*J'aime Mr Smith, je l'aime beaucoup.*'[42] Her novels, so racy and well-written that Marie-Antoinette is said to have disguised them as Books of Hours so she could consult them at Mass,[43] actually invert the sexual hierarchy of the *Theory*. Women are not inferior but superior to men, not merely because of the intensity of their *sensibilité* but because of the immeasurably greater peril they run in matters of love. As one of Mme Riccoboni's heroines writes to her lover, 'the attachment of a delicate woman is above any conception of your sex.'[44]

Among the men, Smith met all the principal theorists concerned with France's commercial policies and primitive finances, such as the tax-farmer Claude-Adrien Helvétius, André Morellet (who was to translate *The Wealth of Nations*) and Anne-Robert-Jacques Turgot, who was to become Controller-General of Finance between 1774 and 1776. 'We spoke of commercial theory, banking, public credit and several points to do with the great work he was cogitating,' the Abbé Morellet wrote, and added: 'He made me a present of a very handsome English pocket-book, as was his custom. I used it for twenty years.'[45] Townshend's appointment in July as Chancellor of the Exchequer – the British equivalent of Controller-General – must have added to Smith's prestige.

He also became intimate with a group of French reforming thinkers, led by the royal physician François Quesnay, known as the *économistes* or, in modern times and in respect of their cult of nature, *physiocrates*. Indeed, before the discovery of the Glasgow lectures on jurisprudence, it was thought that Smith had derived much of the theory worked out in *The Wealth of Nations* from Quesnay. Now in his seventies, Quesnay had circulated in 1758 his *Tableau économique*, an elaborate and quasi-mathematical model of how national prosperity comes about. A pattern of lines and zigzags showed how the products of agriculture, the sole ultimate source of wealth, would in a state of perfect liberty be distrib-uted among the 'productive' classes of landlords and farmers, and the 'unproductive' classes of workmen and merchants.[46] Quesnay's fellow-*économiste*, the marquis de Mirabeau, described the *Tableau* as the third of humanity's great political inventions, after writing and money.[47] It is not a judgement that has worn well.

Now the *Tableau* was precisely the kind of philosophical machine that had so attracted the Adam Smith of the 'Astronomy' and the essay on language. He approved of agriculture, greatly admired the yeoman character and felt that the interests of the landowner coincided with those of the public at large. What Smith could not accept was that only agriculture was productive in the sense both that it was regener-ated by nature each year and that it yielded a surplus over its costs in the form of a rent to the landlord. He refused to represent 'the class of artificers, manufacturers and merchants, as altogether barren and unproductive'.[48] He believed, as did Turgot, that these classes were also sources of surplus. Smith thought Quesnay 'very ingenious and profound' and later told Stewart that he would have dedicated the book to him, had he lived, but he found his system, in the end, too ambitious and speculative. 'That system,' he wrote in *The Wealth of Nations*, 'which represents the produce of land as the sole source of the revenue and wealth of every country, has, so far as I know, never been adopted by any nation, and it at present exists only in the speculations of a few men of great learning and ingenuity in France.'[49]

He had more pressing need for Quesnay than for his agricultural theory. In August 1766, on an excursion to hunt with the King in the forest of Compiègne, the Duke of Buccleuch fell ill with fever. Beside himself with anxiety, Smith repeatedly called on Quesnay, but found that the royal physician, too, was ill and refused to come out. At Smith's third appeal, Quesnay at last agreed to see Buccleuch. Finding the patient in a profuse sweat, Quesnay resolved not to intervene but 'only ordered him some cooling ptisane drink', as Smith reported to Charles Townshend on the 26th. 'I never stirr from his room from eight in the morning till ten at night,' Smith continued, 'and watch for the smallest change that happens to him. I should sit by him at night too, if the ridiculous impertinent jealousy of Cook [Buccleuch's servant], who thinks my assiduity an encroachment upon his duty, had not been so much alarmed as to give some disturbance even to his master in his present illness.'[50]

The Duke recovered, but some time in October, his younger brother Hew also fell ill. Rae reported a tradition that he had been attacked in the street.[51] On 15 October, Smith wrote to the young men's sister, Lady Frances Scott, that Hew was being treated by Dr Richard Gem of the British Embassy and by Quesnay. So alarmed was Smith that he had also called in Dr Tronchin, his 'particular and intimate friend' from Geneva days.[52] His last letter to Lady Frances makes sad reading. He had gone to see the Duke and warn him to expect the worst. 'I returned in less than half an hour to do the last duty to my best friend. He had expired about five minutes before I could get back and I had not the satisfaction of closing his eyes with my own hands. I have no force to continue this letter.'[53]

Smith and the Duke, who was 'in very great affliction', accompanied Hew's body back to Dover, arriving on 1 November.[54] Smith was glad to be back. As he had written to Andrew Millar a week or two before, 'I long passionately to rejoin my old friends, and if I had once got fairly to your side of the water [the English Channel], I think I should never cross it again.'[55] He never did.

What had Smith gained? The snob Alexander Carlyle, who thought Townshend was merely showing off in sending 'an eminent Scotch philosopher to travel with the Duke',[56] was proved wrong. Smith was an excellent tutor. His pupil was turned, as his stepfather Townshend had always intended, into *The Theory of Moral Sentiments* incarnate. In the portrait by Thomas Gainsborough, painted in 1770 or 1771, the Duke wears the insignia of the Order of the Garter and hugs a Dandie Dinmont terrier. He is a young man so assured of his own position and ability that he looks at the viewer with an almost superhuman benevolence. He is a person 'who joins, to the most perfect command of his own original and selfish feelings, the most exquisite sensibility'.[57] Years later, the Duke wrote to Dugald Stewart: 'In October, 1766, we returned to London, after having spent near three years together, without the slightest disagreement or coolness.'[58]

While there is no hint in *The Wealth of Nations* of the threat to public order that was gathering in France like a distant storm, and would burst in 1789, Smith knew both the country and Quesnay well enough to make a detailed and powerful case against oppressive aspects of the *ancien régime* such as the manipulation of the coinage, the uncertainty and arbitrary nature of taxation, the misery of agriculture, and the burdensome public debt. He also gained greatly in urbanity. Ramsay of Ochtertyre said that Smith acquired on his travels a degree of polish and address 'which was hardly to be expected at his time of life'.[59] In both *The Wealth of Nations* and the new section, 'Of the Character of Virtue', that he added to *The Theory of Moral Sentiments*, there is a new elegance to his always lucid style.

Smith spent six months in London, supervising the third edition of the *Theory*, which was composed in new type and bound up with the 'Dissertation on the Origin of Languages'. Letters give glimpses of his reading. On 12 February, he told the second Lord Shelburne that he had spent two days (presumably in the British Museum) studying the colonies of ancient Rome. (He was to write about ancient and modern colonial policy in Book Four of *The Wealth of Nations*.[60]) His intention to settle in London had evaporated. On 25 March, he began shipping his books north. They included Adam Anderson's *Origin of Commerce*,[61] a diary of commercial events from the Creation to 1762 and described by the *Dictionary of National Biography* as 'a monument of stupendous industry'; and Malachi Postlethwayt's *Universal Dictionary of Trade and Commerce*, just issued in a third edition. There must have been many more for Smith insured the shipment for £200.[62] Having done his fundamental reading long ago at college, Smith seems to have busied himself with tracts on the corn trade, taxation and customs, the publications of the French *parlements* and the English and Scottish statutes, and travellers' accounts of North and South America, southern Africa, China, Arabia and Central Asia or, as he called it, Tartary.

The Duke of Buccleuch married in London on 3 May 1767, and some time afterwards Smith set off to join his mother and Janet Douglas in Fife. In a letter to Hume from Kirkcaldy, he wrote: 'My business here is study in which I have been very deeply engaged for about a month past. My amusements are long, solitary walks by the sea side. You may judge how I spend my time. I feel myself, however, extremely happy, comfortable and contented. I never was, perhaps, more so in all my life.'[63] Later that month, he wrote to the Duke's factor to acknowledge receipt of the first payment of his pension.[64] In September, Buccleuch came north for the first time with his bride to celebrate his majority and take over his Scottish estates. Carlyle gives a catty portrait of the philosopher at the Duke's twenty-first birthday party: 'The company was formal and dull. Adam Smith, their only familiar at table, was but ill qualified to promote the jollity of a birthday.' Fortunately, Carlyle himself and an attorney named M'Millan managed to set the toasts going.[65]

Smith was later to describe this period thus: 'I continued to live for six years in great tranquillity, and almost in complete retirement. During this time I amused myself principally with writing my Enquiry concerning the Wealth of Nations, in studying botany (in which however I made no great progress) as well as some other sciences to which I had never given much attention before.'[66] Two substantial Scottish works, Sir James Steuart's *Inquiry into the Principles of Political Oeconomy*, and Adam Ferguson's *Essay on the History of Civil Society*, appeared on ground that Smith had marked out as his own. Early in 1768, Smith wrote to Shelburne that he had not 'made all the progress that I expected', and might need to remain in the north right through until after Christmas. He wrote, as he reminded Shelburne, 'in so bad a hand'.[67]

Christmas 1768 came and went. In the new year, a correspondence of six letters with the Scottish legal antiquary Sir David Dalrymple, lately raised to the bench as Lord Hailes, showed Smith was working on nominal and real prices. On 15 January, he asked for the use of Hailes's papers on historic corn prices, while promising to help Hailes in some of his own arcane legal researches. Far from being near completion, Smith's book was becoming more and more unwieldy. 'My own papers,' he wrote, 'are in very great disorder and I wait for some further informations which I expect from different quarters before I attempt to give them the last arrangement.'[68] Hailes's price survey, culled from the charters and rent rolls of ancient Scottish abbeys and bishoprics, was finally sent on 6 March 1769. Smith combined it with material from English and French sources in the long 'Digression concerning the Variations in the Value of Silver during the Course of the Four Last Centuries' at the end of Book One of *The Wealth of Nations*.

Hume, who had spent two years in London as under-secretary for the Northern Department (that is, Scottish affairs), returned to Edinburgh in the summer of 1769. From his apartment in James' Court in the Lawnmarket he could see across the broad Firth to Kirkcaldy, but his proposals that they meet seem to have come to nothing.[69] A little later, Smith told the attorney John Davidson that 'I shall not [leave] my retreat for above a day these six months.'[70] It was said that, while dictating to his scribe in the study of his mother's house in the High Street, he used to stand with his back to the fire and rub his head against the chimney-breast. Visitors were shown the traces of his pomade well into the nineteenth century.[71]

In 1772, there was further excuse for delay, when a new bank in western Scotland, Douglas, Heron & Co., usually known as the Ayr Bank, collapsed, precipitating a general depression through the Lowlands. The Ayr Bank, which had opened for business on 6 November 1769 with Buccleuch as one of the directors, had financed land speculation by its partners through short-term borrowing at ruinous rates in London.[72] When a London Scottish banking house, Neale, James, Fordyce and Downe, collapsed on 10 June 1772 with liabilities of £243,000, there was a run on the Edinburgh banks and the Ayr Bank, whose balance-sheet had swelled to £1.25m, stopped redeeming its banknotes on 5 June. 'Do these events any-wise affect your theory?' Hume wrote from his new house in the Edinburgh New Town on the 27th. 'Or will it occasion the revisal of any chapters?'[73] That it certainly did, most notably the chapter on 'Money Considered as a particular Branch of the general Stock' in Book Two of *The Wealth of Nations*.

Smith wrote at the height of the crisis to his friend William Pulteney, MP for Cromarty, that he had hoped to have the book ready for the winter, but he had been distracted by the financial uncertainty. 'Tho I had no concern myself in the public calamities, some of the friends for whom I interest myself the most have been deeply concerned in them; and my attention has been a good deal occupied about the most proper method of extracting them.'[74] That appears to be code for Buccleuch.

The bank was forced to offer usurious rates on its annuities in London, but that bought respite only to the spring.[75] Without limited liability, the partners were called on to find more than £600,000. In Edinburgh itself, only the Royal Bank of Scotland, the Bank of Scotland, the British Linen Company and four private houses survived.

The other problem was depression of spirits, or what Smith called 'bad health arising from want of amusement and from thinking too much upon one thing'.[76] Anxious about his friend's welfare, Hume proposed in November that Smith come to live as his neighbour in the new suburbs being built in Edinburgh, now known as the New Town. Hume had an apartment in mind, not far from his own house, with a view down Princes Street, Castle and fields to the west, the sea and even Kirkcaldy to the east, and all for just £35 *per annum*.[77] In a postscript, Hume sent some information on the import of American silver into Spain that he had collected for his essay of 1752, 'Of Money.'

Smith seems to have considered going abroad again, even to India. In the letter to Pulteney of 5 September 1772, Smith thanks his friend 'for having mentioned me to the east India Directors as a person who could be of any use to them'. Pulteney seems to have proposed Smith (among others) as a member of a commission to look into the desperate state of the Indian administration. It came to nothing, though Sir James Steuart, who had at last been pardoned for coming out with Prince Charlie in the 'Forty-five, was invited to report on the particular problem of the coinage in Bengal.

The next suggestion was that Smith might travel abroad as tutor to the young Duke of Hamilton, and he was invited to London to discuss the matter with the young man's mother and guardians. Hume, expecting him in Edinburgh on 10 April 1773, wondered if he was 'pulling down or building up' his great work.[78] Kames, too, talked of Smith 'building and demolishing' in a letter to a Swiss correspondent on 20 April.[79]

Smith's hypochondria was now so acute that he feared he might die in England, and he wrote to Hume before leaving Edinburgh, appointing him literary executor and asking him to destroy his writings, except the manuscript of the new book and the 'Astronomy'. The letter is both formal and curiously intimate. 'All the other loose papers, which you will find either in that desk or within the glass folding doors of a bureau which stands in my bed room together with about eighteen thin paper folio books which you will likewise find within the same glass folding doors I desire may be destroyed without any examination.'[80]

Once in London, he was dissuaded from going abroad by his former pupil, the Duke of Buccleuch.[81] He stayed on in London, no doubt fascinated by the drama unfolding on both sides of the Atlantic. Townshend's revenue policies had their consequences in the famous Boston Tea Party of 16 December 1773, when a group of men dressed as Mohawks dumped dutied tea from India into Boston harbour. A series of retaliatory acts by Lord North's government in London in 1774 convinced the Americans that the mother country was bent on extinguishing their liberties. We know that Smith attended debates in Parliament as the crisis unfolded.

Hume was, as he put it, 'an American in my principles'.[82] He favoured separation not simply because he disapproved of the policies of Lord North's administration but because he thought independence was as natural to a colony as to a growing child. Smith – like Benjamin

Franklin in those days – proposed a closer union or federation, even if that implied that the centre of empire would, in time, move west.[83] He did not believe that it was wrong to tax the American colonies any more than did Charles Townshend. What was wrong was to try to maintain through violence restrictions on their trade of which the trade of the mother country was free, and to deny them representation in proportion to their tax contribution. It is worth remembering that at this time Scotland, with a franchise of little more than 3,000 voters out of a population of over a million people, was not exactly *represented* at Westminster.

As well as writing the section on the American colonies in Book Four, Smith was also gathering material on French and Irish revenue. A long letter to Dr Cullen in September 1774, opposing a university monopoly on medical qualifications, showed that he had already thought through the arguments for free competition in the learned professions that are deployed with such disarming wit in Book Five.[84]

As to his social life, Smith picked up his letters at the British Coffee-House in Suffolk Street, off Charing Cross, which was then popular with the Scots in the capital. He was admitted in May 1773 as a Fellow of the Royal Society, the British academy of science, and two years later to Dr Johnson's famous club. Johnson and Smith never got on. Johnson distrusted Smith's religion, and hated his association with Hume. Smith's tendency either to day-dream or to lecture did not go down well. Johnson declared to Boswell that Smith 'was as dull a dog as he had ever met with'. Boswell, who had received much kindness from Smith as a student at Glasgow, could not now recognise his old moral-philosophy professor in this 'professed Infidel with a bag wig'.[85]

He wrote to his friend William Temple in the West Country: 'Smith too is now of our club. It has lost its select merit.'

On 18 April 1775, British regular troops clashed with American militias at Lexington and Concord. There was little chance now of conciliation. On 9 May, Smith reassured Hume: 'I shall send my own book to the Press in the end of this month or the beginning of the next.'[86] Yet the following November, John Roebuck, a chemical engineer and former partner of James Watt, was still urging Smith to hurry up if he wanted to exercise any influence on events in America. He sent an eye-witness account of the fighting around Boston and added: 'I hoped by this time to have seen your name in the Papers. The meeting of Parliament is the proper time for the publication of a such a work as yours.'[87] Hume was becoming more and more anxious at the silence. 'By all accounts,' he wrote on 8 February 1776, 'your book has been printed long ago; yet it has never yet been so much as advertised. What is the reason? If you wait till the fate of America be decided, you may wait long.'[88]

An Inquiry into the Nature and Causes of the Wealth of Nations, by Adam Smith LL.D and FRS, appeared with Millar's successors in the Strand, William Strahan and Thomas Cadell, on 9 March 1776. It was printed in two volumes quarto, bound in blue or marbled boards, and priced at one pound and sixteen shillings. The book went through five editions in what remained of Smith's life, and was quickly translated into German, French and Danish and then into the other literary languages. *The Wealth of Nations* more or less defined the field of inquiry known as political economy until the late nineteenth century, and continued to influence thinking on taxation, freedom of trade and public education into the twenty-first. The Victorian philosopher Henry Thomas Buckle thought it 'probably the most important book that has ever been written'.[89]

5

Baboons in the Orchard

1776

If the *Theory of Moral Sentiments* analyses the drawing room and parlour, *The Wealth of Nations* takes the reader into the open air. In a fashion that is now commonplace but was then quite new, Smith brought to bear on the chaos of commercial and industrial phenomena that system of cause and effect that philosophers and theologians had applied to appetites and angels.

Behind *The Wealth of Nations*, and just evident beyond the wheat and herring and hearth-taxes, is the ghost of an old-fashioned inquiry into the moral character of luxury. Since the modern societies of the West no longer distinguish between need and wish, luxury or what we would now call consumption beyond animal necessity has lost its philosophical interest. '*Le superflu,*' said Voltaire, '*chose tres nécessaire*';[1] or, in modern English, I'll die if I don't have those shoes.

Yet in antiquity and the Middle Ages, luxury was a mortal threat to body and soul. It sapped the courage of men and the chastity of women. It enervated the state both in its fighting strength and also, because most luxuries came from outside the realm, its treasure. And where would it all lead? 'Alone of all animalls on this globe,' Smith told his students, man ascribes values to qualities such as colour, rarity and shape that give no 'superior advantage in supplying the wants of nature'.[2] He seeks out from the other 'pebbles' diamonds and rubies. Bodily needs can be satisfied but desires, in Smith's beautiful phrase, 'seem to be altogether endless'.[3]

Much *débris* had already been cleared from the philosophical approaches to luxury. The English merchant pamphleteers of the seventeenth century – men such as Sir William Petty, Nicholas Barbon and Sir Dudley North – demonstrated how the luxury trades encouraged industry. 'It is the sensual courtier that sets no limit to his luxury,' wrote Mandeville, 'the fickle strumpet that invents new fashions every week; the haughty dutchess ... the profuse rake and lavish heir ... the covetous and perjur'd villain ... it is these ... that we stand in need of ... to procure an honest livelihood to the vast multitudes of working poor, that are required to make a large society.'[4] Hume declared that modern luxury does not taint character but polishes it. In his essay 'Of Luxury' – renamed 'Of Refinement in the Arts' to remove any taint of censoriousness – improvements in the 'mechanical arts' stimulate refinements in the 'liberal' arts and sciences, men become sociable and women valued, 'and the tempers of men, as well as their behaviour, refine apace. So that, beside the improvements, which they receive from knowledge and the liberal arts, it is impossible but they must feel an encrease of humanity ...'[5] Sir James Steuart saw luxury as the well-spring of activity in free societies, and did not spare the backwoods: 'I am no patron either of vice, profusion, or the dissipation of private fortunes, although I may now and then reason very coolly upon the political consequences of such diseases in a state, when I consider only the influence they have as to feeding and multiplying a people.'[6] These men were experimenting with a new way of seeing things, where the limitlessness of desire, far from being the destruction of the world, is its salvation: the very force that runs through history and makes it intelligible.

As for treasure, who needed it? In 'Of the Balance of Trade', Hume presented a working engine of what modern economists call the specie-flow theory. Bullion, unless it is sterilised in church plate or absorbed by an increase in goods for sale, will drive up the prices of commodities at home and make them unaffordable overseas. As a consequence, the flow of foreign treasure diminishes, prices at home fall, and so on round and round and round. The merchant and landed interests that dominated the British Parliament still insisted that exports should be encouraged and imports discouraged. But that, as Smith was to argue, was a mere reflex to stifle competition and preserve the social hierarchy for their own convenience. 'I have never known much good done by those who affected to trade for the publick good,' he wrote in *The Wealth of Nations*. 'It is an affectation, indeed, not very common among merchants, and very few words need be employed in dissuading them from it.'[7]

So if a prince's treasure was not wealth, what was? Smith's first thoughts on the subject are as crude as tavern signs. 'That state is

opulent,' he said in his lecture of 29 March 1763, 'where the necessaries and conveniencies of life are easily come at, whatever otherwise
be its condition, and nothing else can deserve the name of opulence but
this comeattibleness.'[8] That last word had entered Smith's consciousness by a sort of side-door, for it was coined by Mandeville to describe
the great virtue of prostitutes over honest women.[9] By 13 April, Smith
had exchanged it for the no less homely, but more chaste 'consumptibility'. 'For to what purpose do all those things which a nation possesses
serve? To no other but the maintaining the people. And how is that this
end is answered? By being consumed.'[10] Even treasure must in the end
be consumed, else it is not treasure.

In his lectures, Smith had discussed 'the opulence of a state' under
the old-fashioned French heading of 'police' as part of the 'the inferiour
parts of government, *viz.* cleanliness, security, and cheapness or
plenty'.[11] In the next twelve years, in Quesnay's *entresol* apartment at
Versailles, by the roaring Firth at Kirkcaldy and in the British Museum
in London, Smith dropped this little term for something broader and
more precise. The new heading, borrowed from Sir James Steuart, is
'political economy'.

'Political economy,' Smith writes, 'considered as a branch of the
science of a statesman or legislator proposes two distinct objects: first,
to provide a plentiful revenue or subsistence for the people, or more
properly to enable them to provide such a revenue or subsistence for
themselves; and secondly, to supply the state or commonwealth with
a revenue sufficient for the publick services.' In the next sentence,
he prescribes the panacea of every Scots financier and charlatan
since John Law of Lauriston had won over the French Regency to

paper money in 1715: 'It proposes to enrich both the people and the sovereign.'[12]

How was it that the world had gained in prosperity? How was it, as Voltaire had put it, that it cost little more to live in comfort under Louis XV in the eighteenth century than in discomfort under Henri IV in the sixteenth?[13] 'The poor labourer,' Smith said in his lecture of 29 March 1763, 'bears on his shoulders the whole of mankind, and unable to sustain the load is buried by the weight of it and thrust down into the lowest part of the earth, from whence he supports all the rest. In what manner then shall we account for the great share he and the lowest of the people have of the conveniencies of life.'[14]

The answer is not the silver of Peru, nor the wisdom of the sovereign nor the discoveries of philosophers, but an instinctive form of industrial organisation: 'The division of labour amongst different hands can alone account for this.' To illustrate specialisation in modern industry, Smith abandoned Mandeville's example of the labourer's woollen coat,[15] which he had borrowed for the 'Early Draft', in favour of an object so trifling as to be provocative: the pin. (Socrates was chided in Athens for a demeaning interest in 'smiths, cobblers and tanners'.[16] Smith would certainly have known that.)

The article *épingle* in the *Encyclopédie* of 1755 had identified eighteen separate operations in the manufacturing of pins, and that was the starting-point for Smith's excursion:

One man draws out the wire, another straights it, a third cuts it, a fourth points it, a fifth grinds it at the top for receiving the head; to make the head requires two or three distinct operations; to put it on, is a peculiar business, to whiten the pins is another; it is even a trade by itself to put them into the paper; and the important business of making a pin is, in this manner, divided into about eighteen distinct operations, which, in some manufactories, are all performed by distinct hands, though in the others the same man will sometimes perform two or three of them. I have seeen a small manufactory of this kind where ten men only were employed, and where some of them consequently performed two or three distinct operations. But though they were very poor, and therefore but indifferently accommodated with the necessary machinery, they could, when they exerted themselves make among them about twelve pounds of pins in a day. There are in a pound upwards of four thousand pins of a middling size. Those ten persons, therefore, could make among them upwards of forty-eight thousand pins ... But if they had all wrought separately and independently, and without any of them having been educated to this peculiar business, they could not each of them have made twenty, perhaps not one pin in a day.[17]

The higher output creates a surplus over what is necessary to train, feed and house the workers, furnish their materials and tools, and satisfy their employers. While the pins become cheaper, wages and profits and rents do not fall but rise. If that sounds like opulence, it must be.

This division of labour, which is to *The Wealth of Nations* what sympathy is to *The Theory of Moral Sentiments*, was no discovery of Adam Smith. Seventeenth-century thinkers, such as Sir William Petty, recognised that specialisation increased the productive powers of human work. 'Cloth must be cheaper made,' he wrote, 'when one cards, another spins, another weaves ... than when all the Operations above-mentioned, were clumsily performed by the same hand.'[18] For Mandeville, the fitting out and manning of a first-rate man-of-war 'would be impracticable, if it were not divided and subdivided into a great variety of different labours'.[19] Hume identified the 'partition of employments' as one of the three great benefits delivered to the individual by living in society.[20]

It was understood in the ancient world. 'Quantity and quality,' Plato had written in *The Republic*, 'are therefore more easily produced when a man specialises on a single job for which he is fitted by nature and ignores all others.'[21] But, as Smith had argued in his lectures,[22] such specialisation would not deliver improvements if the artisans were slaves whose labour and innovations belonged to their masters. What was needed was freedom, which now enters *The Wealth of Nations*, not as the sunny mental tranquillity of those Stoic beggars by the roadside, but as freedom of *occupation*. Provided they are free to do so, and they are safe and feel safe, men set up in different trades, according to their skills and preferences. For Smith, unlike snobs such as Voltaire, men are born with more or less equal gifts, and their different aptitudes are the *effect* not the *cause* of the division of labour. Long ago, as he marched up the Edinburgh High Street past the Highland caddies lounging at mid-day by the Cross, Adam Smith made up his mind. There was little to no difference at birth or for the first six or eight years of life 'between a philosopher and a common street porter'.[23]

What gives rise to the division of labour? It is not the product of ideal wisdom, as in Plato, or God-given and eternal as in medieval Christendom and Hindu India, but springs from a propensity to 'truck, barter, and exchange one thing for another'.[24] This propensity is natural to man and man alone among animals. 'Nobody ever saw a dog make a fair and deliberate exchange of one bone for another with another dog.' Even if, as travellers reported, baboons co-operated in robbing orchards at the Cape of Good Hope, they fought to the death over the spoils.[25]

Why man should enjoy this propensity, and not dogs and baboons, Smith does not enquire. Smith had taken truck-and-barter from the Latin of the Dutch jurist Hugo Grotius and does nothing with it except to say that it may be the 'necessary consequence of the faculty of reason and speech'. Even the rhetorical anthropology of the *Lectures* – that exchange arises in 'the natural inclination every one has to persuade'[26] – has fallen away.

It is a brittle foundation for a philosophical edifice. As ever, what appear to be first principles are, as John Stuart Mill put it, last principles: 'though presented as if all other truths were to be deduced from them, they are the truths which are last arrived at.'[27] Rather, Smith is signalling that he is not to be diverted from his commercial purpose by his old moral, rhetorical and aesthetic interests. Those he will return to in time.

Commerce grows and spreads not for love of God or fear of the ruler or from some fabulous Hutchesonian benevolence, but out of co-operative self-interest. 'Give me that which I want,' Smith writes, 'and you shall have this which you want ... it is in this manner that we obtain from one another the far greater part of those good offices which we stand in need of. It is not from the benevolence of the butcher, the brewer, or the baker, that we expect our dinner, but from their regard to their own interest.'[28] This then is the 'mercenary exchange of good offices according to an agreed valuation', a subsidiary actor in *The Theory of Moral Sentiments*, now brought to philosophical centre-stage.[29]

The division of labour cannot function without a market for its specialities. A street porter would never find work enough in a village, but must migrate to the Cross of Edinburgh. As markets become more extended – say, through water-carriage in the canals just now being cut through Scotland and England – so there is further specialisation and further gains in productivity and further output of commodities. These commodities (or services) need to be exchanged and Smith proceeds to barter and then, because that is inconvenient and inexact, money, gold and silver, coinage, paper, banking and public credit.

Smith gives a 'philosophical' account of the origins of money. His history does not correspond to the documentary history of money, which Smith did not know nor, one imagines, very much care to find out. Even now, after two hundred years of archaeology and scientific ethnography, the origins and ancient history of money are a riddle. So, for other reasons, are values expressed in money – prices – but here Smith is in his element.

Real and nominal prices, a commonplace after the twentieth-century inflations, were not well understood in the eighteenth century. Though men measured their wages in the money they received, Smith explained, their real prosperity or welfare varied according to the volume or quality of goods that money could command. Whatever, for example, the spendthrift French monarchy did to the nominal value of the coin, the volume of goods it would buy would, after some disruption, revert to the old quantity. Moreover, those goods are just a synonym for the work put into them. At this moment, as he presents his labour theory of value, Smith is momentarily distracted by a paradox: that water, the most useful of all substances, is priced at but a fraction of diamond, which has almost no use.[30] With his new philosophical self-control, he hurries on.

Instead, Smith shows that there are two sorts of prices in a commodity or object for sale. There is its price in the market which is governed by how many people want it and how badly, and something he calls natural price. In the *Lectures*, this natural price was the sum of the cost to the producer of his materials and a surplus to train him up and keep him and his family fed. Should the price of his product fall below this natural price, he will starve or try to move to another occupation. His departure, one way or the other, will cause the natural price of the abandoned product to rise, another producer will take it up, and so on.

In the more advanced society of *The Wealth of Nations*, this producer now works for somebody else on ground that is not his own. The natural price must now pay not just a living wage but also a profit to his employer. This is a reward not just for management – 'the labour of inspection and direction'[31] – but for assembling the components of production. Finally, in a world where 'men love to reap where they never sowed',[32] proprietors or landlords demand a rent for the use of their land or they will not let it out.

Wages, profit and rent are, in the manner of the *économistes* and Turgot, both categories of revenue and the badges of distinct orders or classes of men and women. 'In the price of corn, for example,' Smith writes, 'one part pays the rent of the landlord, another pays the wages or maintenance of the labourers and the labouring cattle employed in producing it, and the third pays the profit of the farmer.'[33] It is as if these three classes were Estates to replace the superannuated nobility, clergy and commons of the *ancien régime*. They are the 'three great, original and constituent orders of every civilized society, from whose revenue that of every other order is derived'.[34]

These classes of revenue and occupation wish to perpetuate themselves. The business person or 'undertaker', in pursuit of gain, makes the most efficient distribution of materials among his workmen, who seeking to better their condition and provide for themselves a comfortable retirement, seek out the most rewarding employments, which ensure a return to the landlord that makes it worth his while to let his ground. This is scientific, even Newtonian. 'The natural price, therefore, is, as it were, the central price, to which the prices of all commodities are continually gravitating.'[35]

For this system to adjust and find its level or equilibrium, there must be more than a relatively extensive market and some money to make it work. The producer must be free to choose his occupation. Market and natural prices will only coincide 'where there is perfect liberty, or where he may change his trade as often as he pleases'.[36] Yet everywhere were artificial impediments such as corporation or guild privileges, gruelling statutes of apprenticeship, or old-fashioned settlement laws that barred a labourer from moving parish, and even, in parts of Scotland, remnants of indentured slavery. Because these restrictions maintained the market price above the natural price, they were impolitic. Because they violated the 'sacred property' a man has in his own labour, they were unjust.[37] (Smith argued for high labourers' wages, because he thought they encouraged hard work, marriage and the welfare of children. Those are, however, subsidiary arguments: 'It is but equity, besides, that they who feed, cloath and lodge the whole body of the people, should have such a share of the produce of their own labour as to be themselves tolerably well fed, cloathed and lodged.'[38])

Likewise, Smith attacks laws or customs of primogeniture and entail, monopolies and combinations and the rigmarole of prohibitions, duties and export bounties that artificially raised market prices. For all the talk of English liberty, many of these restrictions and privileges had been entrenched for centuries, while many trades were intent on devising new monopolies and restrictions. 'People of the same trade seldom meet together, even for merriment and diversion, but the conversation ends in a conspiracy against the publick, or in some contrivance to raise prices.'[39] Once again, monopolies and combinations are attacked on grounds of efficiency – as enemies to good management[40] – and only then on grounds of equity.

The first book ends, after a long digression on historical prices, with a warning against the sectional power of merchants and manufacturers. Of the three 'great, original and constituent orders', the landed men are generally too indolent and the labourers too weak to do much to injure the interest of society as a whole. Not so the merchants, who are constantly looking for ways to increase profit, and are more alert than the landlords and better educated than the workmen. 'The proposal of any new law or regulation of commerce' that arises from the merchant class, therefore, 'ought always to be listened to with great precaution'.[41]

The second book of *The Wealth of Nations* returns to the division of labour and reminds the reader that a specialist producer, such as a weaver, must accumulate 'a stock of goods' or he will starve before he has sold his cloth. This stock, which began life in the *Lectures* as a legal category of household property, is the remunerative property not only of an individual, but of an employer of several individuals and even of the state. It is what we now call capital, which enters the scene as the third actor – after specialisation and freedom of occupation – in the drama. The section is strongly influenced by French thought.

Just as the workman can consume part of his stock or set it to earn him income so, by analogy, the capital of any 'country or society' may be so allocated. The remunerative property Smith divides, like the *économistes*, into the money and goods that earn revenue only by changing hands, like the stock in trade of a shopkeeper. That he calls circulating capital. It differs from fixed capital, such as machines and tools, warehouses and factories and improved farmland, which earns revenue without changing hands. For Smith, fixed capital was any investment that increased 'the productive powers of labour'[42] and that included the 'useful abilities' acquired by the workman through education and apprenticeship.[43]

It is the interplay of circulating and fixed capital, in conditions of relative freedom and security, which is at the heart of Smith's *tableau économique*. In its daily purchases, the public withdraws from the circulating capital of society, which must then be replaced through additional raw materials from agriculture and finished goods from manufacture.

Smith breaks with the *économistes* in rejecting any privilege for agriculture. Both sectors are productive. 'Land, mines, and fisheries,'

Smith writes, 'require all both a fixed and circulating capital to cultivate them; and their produce replaces with a profit, not only those capitals, but all the others in the society. Thus the farmer annually replaces to the manufacturer the provisions which he had consumed and the materials which he had wrought up the year before; and the manufacturer replaces to the farmer the finished work which he had wasted and worn out in the same time.' With a bow to the shade of Quesnay, he continues: 'This is the real exchange which is annually made between these two orders of people.'

For all Smith's suspicion of sectional interests, here is none of that class antagonism that Karl Marx drew from his readings of Steuart and Ferguson, but rather a visionary interdependence, which seems to come out of some medieval Book of Hours, done up for the commercial age. 'Land even replaces, in part, at least, the capitals with which fisheries and mines are cultivated. It is the produce of land which draws the fish from the waters; and it is the produce of the surface of the earth which extracts the minerals from its bowels.'[44]

Smith moves on to make some ingenious suggestions for increasing fixed capital while reducing, through such banking innovations as the Bank of England or the Scottish paper money, the cost of circulating capital. A merchant's ready money or cash balances are so much dead stock in that they do no work for him. So is the money of the realm. It is as if, as Smith put it in the *Lectures* and the 'Early Draft', all the arable land and pasture were overrun with highways to transport corn and hay. Groping for a metaphor to express this novel idea, Smith struck gold. He writes: 'The judicious operations of banking, by providing ... a sort of waggon-way through the air; enable the country to convert, as it were, a great part of its highways into good pastures and corn fields, and thereby to increase very considerably the annual produce of its land and labour.'[45]

In the next chapter, Smith shows just how his analysis demolishes cherished illusions about *ancien régime* society. There *is* a distinction between productive and unproductive labour but it is not as the good Dr Quesnay thought. The distinction is not between farmers and manufacturers but between those who produce work that perpetuates itself and those who, while producing something of value, must be maintained by the work of other people. In a passage provocative even by his own elevated standard, Smith includes in the unproductive class kings, judges, the army and Royal Navy, domestic servants, 'churchmen, lawyers, physicians, men of letters of all kinds; players, buffoons, musicians, opera-singers, opera-dancers, etc.'.[46]

Adam Smith was no economic philistine. He loved the theatre and music and dancing, thought them the most natural of pursuits[47] and a necessary medicine against the disease of religious fanaticism.[48] Yet the labour of these artists 'perishes in the very instant of its production'. A general or admiral may save the nation this year, but his exploit will not inevitably protect it from defeat next year. Smith casts up his thought into an aphorism: 'A man grows rich by employing a multitude of manufacturers [i.e. makers of things for sale]. He grows poor by maintaining a multitude of menial servants.'[49] Hume believed, with his habitual good nature, that 'the same age, which produces great philosophers and politicians, renowned generals and poets, usually abounds with skilful weavers and ship-carpenters.'[50] Smith believed, and experience seconds him, that a society does well to mingle with its politicians and poets one or two weavers and ship-carpenters.

What unites us all, productive and unproductive, is the desire of 'bettering our condition', which proceeds 'in spite both of the extravagance of government, and of the greatest errors of administration'. What the phrase 'bettering our condition' means in conditions of luxury and superfluity is not at all clear, but almost certainly not very much. Smith takes refuge in assertion. 'An augmentation of fortune is the means by which the greater part of men propose and wish to better their condition.' And how is that done? 'It is the means the most vulgar and the most obvious ... to save and accumulate some part of what they acquire.' This 'principle of frugality seems not only to predominate, but to predominate very greatly'.[51] However blustery the argument, it does at least render 'natural' the third element of Smith's system, capital, which now takes on a secret life of its own, 'silently and gradually accumulated by the private frugality and good conduct of individuals' despite 'all the exactions of government'.[52]

The book continues with a discussion of the relative productivity of capitals, beginning with agriculture, followed by manufacturing and then the wholesale and retail businesses. Smith's preference for agriculture may seem perverse for he had disposed of the *économistes* and conceded that it was an occupation where the division of labour could not be so advanced.[53] Yet at this period, before the dawn of the age of machines, agriculture was a dynamic activity. Farmers were seeing striking increases in agricultural yield through the intelligent application, first in the English county of Norfolk and then in Scotland, of novel techniques of cropping and animal husbandry brought over from the Low Countries. Almost everbody in the intellectual Scottish Lowlands – Kames, Hutton, Steuart, Lord Monboddo, William Cullen, John

Home, Alexander Carlyle – was farming away in the Norfolk style or at least dabbling in it. For Smith, unlike his townee friend Hume, the country gave pleasure and peace of mind and also, what he valued more highly than anything else on earth, 'independency'.[54]

By now, Smith's theory resembles nothing so much as a steam-engine, or as he would call it a 'fire-engine', thudding away with its burnished copper boiler and nodding cross-beam in some European museum of science. He now alters course. As in *The Theory of Moral Sentiments*, Smith exchanges his analytical for a historical approach. Some countries were more advanced in the division of labour and richer in invested capital, and Smith now tries to account for the different rates of what he calls 'the progress of opulence'. In terms of mere logic, the third and fourth books of *The Wealth of Nations* should precede the first and second. In a fashion that is both perverse and also quintessentially eighteenth century, deductions from a hypothetical law of nature precede an investigation of actual historical facts.

It is all the more strange since Smith soon announces that the facts, once they have been assembled, are a distortion or inversion of nature's intended plan. According to the theory laid out in Books One and Two, capital will find its way to those uses which create for societies the greatest prosperity, starting with agriculture, then manufacture, then foreign trade. Drawing on his deep knowledge of Roman and feudal history, and on Hume's *History of England* for more modern times, Smith shows how since the fall of the Roman Empire the towns in Europe had come to dominate the country and not *vice versa*. Agriculture had suffered under feudal service, short leases, primogeniture, strict entail (which covered as much as a third of the land of Scotland),[55] and the violence that bedevilled the countryside.[56] In contrast, the free cities, secure behind their walls, became sanctuaries for capital, markets for manufactured refinements and foreign luxuries, and homes of good government. In time, these amenities spread out into the countryside.

The varied experience of different countries towards 'opulence' had given rise to different theories of political economy. These Smith simplifies in Book Four into two main systems: one that advocates the priority of commerce, the other of agriculture. Under the first or townee system, which he calls the commercial or mercantile, Smith deploys his rhetorical gifts to lampoon old notions that wealth derives from a positive balance of trade made manifest in holdings of gold and silver. He criticises artificial policies to improve the balance through restrictions and preferences, bounties on corn, the re-export preferences known as drawbacks, and other limits to the free movement of capital and working people. In vivid language, he portrays the mercantile interest that dominated the House of Commons as 'like an overgrown standing army' ever poised to intimidate the legislature. He accepts that the sudden opening of a protected market would have drastic effects on both undertakers and workers and, for reasons of 'humanity', such changes should be introduced only 'slowly, gradually, and after a very long warning'. Meanwhile, there were practical limits. 'To expect, indeed, that the freedom of trade should ever be entirely restored in Great Britain, is as absurd as to expect that an Oceana or Utopia [i.e. an ideal commonwealth] should ever be established in it.'[57]

It is in this book that the Invisible Hand makes its last non-appearance. Smith is talking about how the merchant prefers, all other things being equal, to deploy his capital under his eye at home rather than out of sight overseas. The consequence is one he never intended, which is 'to render the annual revenue of society as great as he can'. Though he is looking only for security and gain for himself, 'he is in this, as in many other cases, led by an invisible hand to promote an end which was no part of his intention.'[58]

Smith and his circle loved the paradoxes of unintended consequences. For Adam Ferguson, 'nations stumble upon establishments, which are indeed the result of human action but not the execution of any human design.'[59] Voltaire wrote: 'I rather share the opinion of the Englishman, who said all origins, all laws, all institutions, are like a plum pudding: the first person put in the flour, the next added the eggs, a third the sugar, a fourth the raisins; and so we have plum pudding.'[60] *The Wealth of Nations* is a repetitive book and a mirror passage later in Book Four on the home and foreign trade substitutes for Invisible Hand 'the private interests and passions of individuals'.[61] The magical or mumbo-jumbo element that has so entranced economists is there replaced by ordinary human faculties.

Smith also ridicules attempts by European manufacturers to extend their destructive monopolies to colonies such as Ireland, India and America. In matters of trade, Smith was on the side of the American colonists in their quarrel with King George and his ministers. His arguments, as usual, commence in expediency and end in justice. By encouraging the export of raw materials (or 'rude produce') but not manufactured goods from these possessions, and by diverting capital from the European and entrepôt trade, Britain both hampered its own manufacturing and saddled itself with the costs of colonial administration. Meanwhile, 'to prohibit a great people, however, from making all that they can of every part of their own produce, or from employing their stock and industry in the way that they judge most advantageous to themselves, is a manifest violation of the most sacred right of mankind.'[62] With a clairvoyance remarkable for the year 1776, Smith saw what was to become the United States far eclipsing the mother country in trade and power. 'Such has hitherto been the rapid progress of that country in wealth, population and improvement,' he wrote, 'that in the course of little more than a century, perhaps, the produce of American might exceed that of British taxation. The seat of the empire would then naturally remove itself to that part of the empire which contributed most to the general defence and support of the whole.'[63] Smith thought highly of these arguments, for he was later to speak, with some justice, of the 'very violent attack I had made upon the whole commercial system of Great Britain'.[64] In contrast, for all his respect for Quesnay, the agricultural system of the *économistes* receives scant treatment.

Once these systems of preference and restraint are removed, 'the obvious and simple system of natural liberty establishes itself of its own accord. Every man, as long as he does not violate the laws of justice, is left perfectly free to pursue his own interest his own way, and to bring both his industry and capital into competition with those of any other man, or order of men.'[65] This vision of perfect liberty leaves the sovereign (prince or parliament) with only three duties: the protection of society from invasion from abroad; the establishment and exact administration of justice; and certain public works and institutions that would be unprofitable for private citizens, either individually or in small groups. Such public duties, if carried out to the letter, leave the people scope to 'provide such a revenue or subsistence for themselves'.[66]

Even so, these public works have a cost and require a revenue. Book Five is a discussion of how those revenues should be raised and spent on defence, justice and public works. In matters of defence, Smith takes issue with those Scots thinkers of the seventeenth century, such as Andrew Fletcher, who saw standing armies as mere Praetorian thugs in the making. He also annoyed many of his circle (such as Alexander Carlyle and Adam Ferguson) who wanted a Scottish militia to demonstrate to the world that Scotland was a full partner in union with England. Smith, who like many Scotsmen of his social class had wide connexions with military officers, was able to see that an American militia, once it had served long enough to achieve military discipline, might be a match for the redcoats.[67] The old republican notion that commerce saps the fighting spirit of a nation, still evident in the *Lectures*, has fallen away.

The section on justice is so summary that we can only assume that in the mid-1770s Smith really thought he should save himself for his projected book on jurisprudence. Justice develops, as in the *Lectures*, as society progresses through four stages, from the age of hunters to that of shepherds and then farmers and now merchants. Property becomes entrenched, inequalities arise in possession, society fissures into strata, and institutions of law and order entrench property and authority. 'Civil government,' Smith declares, 'so far as it is instituted for the security of property, is in reality instituted for the defence of the rich against the poor, or of those who have some property against those who have none at all.'[68] No wonder, in the years after the French Revolution, the liberal youth of Edinburgh 'lived upon' Adam Smith.[69]

On public works, Smith argues that public investments to facilitate commerce should be provided only where private individuals have failed. They should be paid for by those that use them so that the bridge or road will be built where it is needed, and to a suitable scale. 'A great bridge,' Smith writes, 'cannot be thrown over a river at a place where nobody passes, or merely to embellish the view from the windows of a neighbouring palace.'[70] (Or, we would add, of a Town or City Hall.) 'Publick services,' as Smith had said in the matter of judges' remuneration, 'are never better performed than when their reward comes only in consequence of their being performed, and is proportioned to the diligence employed in performing them.'[71]

What truly interested Smith was education, and particularly the education of the poor. Smith and his friends such as Kames and Ferguson, and his pupil Millar, were convinced that the division of labour created specialised idiots, men 'mutilated and deformed'[72] in their intellectual faculties by making 'the 17th part of a pin or the 80th part of a button'.[73] Public education, even if it brought the state no advantage, makes the people less open to the political contagion of faction and sedition, fanaticism and superstition. Smith advocated not simply 'parish schools' of the Scottish type but even compulsory education for all children, a professional examination for the labouring classes, and science and philosophy for those of 'middling or more than middling rank and fortune'.[74]

In his discussion of universities, we see the trace left in Smith's nature by his melancholy and isolation at Oxford, but now incorporated into his theory. The problem at the old universities was that the professors did not have to compete for their pupils. As a result, Smith writes, 'in the university of Oxford, the greater part of the publick professors, have for these many years, given up altogether even the pretence of teaching.'[75]

Smith also spares a thought, not a good thought but the only such in *The Wealth of Nations*, for the female population. Because there is no public education for girls, he writes, 'there is accordingly nothing useless, absurd, or fantastical in the common course of their education.' That must have been news to Smith's eighteenth-century readers, but he carries blithely on. 'Every part of their education tends evidently to some useful purpose; either to improve the natural attractions of their person, or to form their mind to reserve, to modesty, to chastity, and to oeconomy; to render them both likely to become the mistresses of a family, and to behave properly when they have become such.'[76]

According to the bill submitted by her boarding school in Edinburgh for the period 14 February to 11 August 1788, a girl from Forfarshire spent on the theatre, coaches, sedan chairs, riding lessons, the races at Leith, gowns, hair, ribbons and frills some £47/3s/9d sterling; enough to maintain a labourer's family in Edinburgh in a respectable condition for three years.[77] So much for female reserve and oeconomy in eighteenth-century Scotland. For conditions in London and Paris, multiply the sum by four. The truth is that women and girls were gathered up in the same cycle of 'consumptibility' as men and, in our age, children. On the credit side, Smith was able at least to steer clear of the debates over female extravagance that were such a feature of the eighteenth century from the days of *The Spectator* and *The Rape of the Lock*.

Instead, Smith's anti-clericalism, reinforced by plentiful quotation from the demon Hume, is deployed against the two bugbears of enthusiasm and supersitition.

Smith recognised that public services could not be maintained without some general taxation and its anticipation through borrowing, and those form the subject of the last two chapters. Tax for Smith was a badge not of slavery, but of liberty,[78] but only if it was collected on principles of equality, certainty, convenience and economy.[79] He was particularly anxious that taxes be levied without impinging on the freedom and privacy of the subject, and without what Quesnay used to call *vexations personnelles*. Though taxes and customs and excise duties must do nothing to disrupt the allocation of capital and work in his theoretical machine, Smith makes enough exceptions to please even a modern Chancellor or Finance Minister. He approves particular taxes on land to influence cultivation, duties to discourage ale-shops or strong drink, sumptuary taxes on luxuries, subsidies on the transport of coal. Taxation should be what is now called 'progressive', in that the rich should pay a higher proportion of their income than the poor. Monopolists certainly should pay on their monopoly profits.[80] In general, Smith prefers taxes on luxuries rather than necessities, while recognising that the distinction was losing its meaning. Why, for example, were shoes a necessity to poor Scotsmen but a luxury to their wives and daughters?[81] As for public borrowing, it is a diversion of productive capital into unproductive projects or warfare, and is often – as modern public creditors know – paid back in a debased or inflated currency.[82] These two fine chapters profit greatly from examples from France.

So Smith comes to his peroration, as cool and powerful an

assault on colonialism as any modern could wish. Taking up the threads of his argument, of the interplay of specialisation, liberty and saving, the progress of history and the recommendations to ministers, Smith returns to the topical political issues of India and America. Since the colonies either cannot or will not pay for their own support and defence, and the monopoly trade is no help but a hindrance, Smith urges Britain to wake from her 'golden dream' of empire and 'endeavour to accommodate her future views and designs to the real mediocrity of her circumstances'.[83]

The most important review was soon in the post. Hume wrote from Edinburgh on 1 April, concealing his diffidence in Greek and Latin. 'Euge! Belle! Dear Mr Smith: I am much pleas'd with your perform-ance, and the perusal of it has taken me from a state of great anxiety.' Hume thought that such a long book would be a challenge to a public with short attention, 'but it has depth and solidity and acuteness, and is so much illustrated by curious facts, that it must at last take the public attention.'[84] Hugh Blair, professor of literature at Edinburgh University, writing two days later, was just as generous and percep-tive. 'You have done great service to the world by overturning all that interested sophistry of merchants, with which they have confounded the whole subject of commerce.' He sided with Smith in his criticism of the universities and if he objected to the passages on the Church, it was for reasons typical of the Moderate churchmen: Smith was *too* favourable to Presbytery, which was both too popular and too austere.[85] Joseph Black praised Smith's 'just and liberal sentiments'.[86] Principal William Robertson, in a letter which must have irritated Smith, was pleased to see his own ideas on the colony trade 'established much better than I could have done myself'.[87] Echoing Blair, he suggested that the book would become a sort of commercial code and would profit from a better index. The pugnacious Ferguson was delighted that Smith had 'provoked ... the church, the universities and the merchants' but took issue, as expected, with Smith's thoughts on the militia.[88]

There were dissenters. The self-conscious Hellenist Lord Monboddo complained about Smith's unclassical style.[89] Alexander Carlyle found the book 'tedious and full of repetition'.[90] The captious and pedantic Governor Pownall failed to find the first principles he was seeking: *'principia'*, to borrow Newton's word, 'to the knowledge of politick operations; as mathmaticks are to mechanicks, astronomy, and the other sciences'.[91]

A better explanation for the book's success came from Edmund Burke in his review in the *Annual Register*. Up to then the rise and decay of nations had been a theme for moralists and politicians. *The Wealth of Nations*, in contrast, offered a 'compleat analysis of society' not only for arts and commerce, but finance, justice, public police, 'oeconomy of armies' and systems of education.[92]

It is not simply that Smith took on a formless mass of commercial thinking and made a system of it, for so did Sir James Steuart's admirable *Principles of Political Oeconomy* of 1767[93] and that was a 'dead dog' long before Karl Marx pronounced it so.[94] Likewise, the works of 'philosophical history' of the Edinburgh circle that correspond to Books Three and Four, such as Kames's *Sketches of the History of Man* of 1774, and the 'View of the Progress of Society in Europe' in Robertson's *History of the Reign of Charles V* (1769). Only Ferguson's

Essay on the History of Civil Society (1767), which found a foothold in Germany, still has readers in scores.

Now Steuart was never forgiven for coming out for Prince Charlie in 1745, and Whig critics disliked his old-fashioned, Continental faith in the wisdom of a prince, or what he was obliged to call in later editions 'the legislature and supreme power'. Smith, in portraying government as little more than a drudge for unprofitable public works, caught the spirit of Whig England and revolutionary America. When Steuart waded into a debate in Glasgow in 1777 on the Corn Laws, he found the partisans of free importation had covered their flank with a 'tremendous piece of ordnance': *The Wealth of Nations*.[95] (In the Spanish epitome, which appeared without Smith's name in 1792, the translator argues that in some countries (i.e. Spain and its possessions) the government not merchants should direct the deployment of capital.[96])

Here, after a century of theorising on law, government and private morality, was something new and comprehensive, full of up-to-date information, and all just in time for the extraordinary experiments in free trade that began with William Pitt the Younger and have continued, with long interruptions, to our own day. It was picked up by men and women who were well informed and up to date. Robert Burns, the poet, who read through the book on his farm in 1789, wrote that: 'I could not have given any mere *man*, credit for half the intelligence Mr Smith discovers [i.e. displays] in his book.'[97]

Now there is much in *The Wealth of Nations* for a modern reader to fault: the reckless *a priori* argument originating in untested propositions; the unsound commercial anthropology; the disdain for mere fact; the parade of dead laws, forgotten excises and superannuated commodities, from the price of a quarter of wheat in 1349 to the tonnage of white herring caught in British waters in 1771; the desert of celibate print without so much as the flutter of a petticoat.

Smith excludes from his theory of opulence any role to increases in population, innovation or the entrepreneur. His world is static, even frozen. One has no sense of population, whether rising or falling, or of that bane of his own and our age, the unemployment or underemployment of the population. Innovation is for Smith mere piecemeal adjustments in the workplace. From hints in the *Lectures* and the 'Early Draft', it seems Smith was working towards a notion of some Promethean philosopher-inventor, a Thomas Edison or William B. Gates.[98] Yet the entrepreneur, the hero of modern economists, is dismissed as a mere 'projector' as likely as not to waste scarce capital on unremunerative schemes.[99]

In his efforts to organise discordant and jarring commercial appearances into a coherent whole and dismiss commercial superstition, Smith gave in to that excessive systematisation that he knew was his philosophical weakness: 'the inclination we naturally have to square and compleat everything, even when by this means we stretch the originall constitution'.[100] The modern reader looks in vain for much sense of the consequence of all this opulence on the natural world. Where is that botany and natural history with which Smith occupied odd hours at Kirkcaldy? Can 'perfect liberty' have much meaning in the age of advertising where vast industries prosper through persuading the public it needs what producers happen to be producing? What happened to the rhetorician in Adam Smith and the philosopher of fashion? As for money, which makes a relation between the most diverse and fortuitous objects and sensations and must merit at least a thought or two in the philosophy of modernity, Smith compares it to a kitchen utensil.[101] Since then, economists have behaved like dogs in the philosophical manger, demanding a monopoly of thought on money, without actually doing any thinking about it.

Yet the personality, as it were, of *The Wealth of Nations* is beguiling: modest, generous and urbane, with the occasional hint of wistfulness or acid. Sir James Steuart is forever struggling to find formulations for his new ideas. He writes in an unhappy mixture of Latinised Scots and Germanised English. One aches to assist him. With Smith, idea and formulation are inextricably intertwined. London and France had refined his style.

In describing in the *Lectures* how the onset of luxury and money broke down the old feudal order, for example, Smith explained how lords exchanged an entourage of tenants for the certainty of a money rent. 'Thus they lost a man for 10 or 5 sh. [shillings], which they spent in follies and luxury.'[102] Thirteen years later, Smith discovers in this piece of history something both comic and desperately sad. 'For a pair of diamond buckles perhaps, or for something as frivolous and useless, they exchanged the maintenance ... of a thousand men for a year, and with it the whole weight and authority which it could give them.' Then, if that phrase were not work enough for a day, the next one is better: 'The buckles, however, were to be all their own.'[103]

6

The Forlorn Station

1776–1790

With his theory out of the way, Smith could now attend to his poor friend David, who was losing ground by the day. In the spring of 1775, as Hume later wrote in the autobiographical fragment entitled 'My Own Life', he had been struck with 'a disorder in my bowels, which at first gave me no alarm, but has since, as I apprehend it, become mortal and incurable'.[1] Within the year, he had lost seventy pounds. To literary diagnosticians, the symptoms have suggested a cancer of the bowel.[2]

On 4 January 1776, Hume drew up his will, appointing Smith his literary executor and leaving him a legacy of £200. He was well enough to read both Edward Gibbon's *Decline and Fall of the Roman Empire* and *The Wealth of Nations* when they arrived in Scotland by the post, but by the time he came to write to Smith in congratulation on 1 April, he was urging him to hurry. 'For I am in a very bad state of health and cannot afford a long delay.'[3] Dr Black reinforced the call to haste, 'that he may have the comfort of your company so much the sooner'.[4]

Black asked Smith to pass on a lengthy diagnosis to Sir John Pringle, a Scots medical doctor in London who was also President of the Royal Society. In the deep past, Pringle had been professor of moral philosophy at Edinburgh and, when he resigned in 1745 to act as Physician-general to the British army in Flanders, Hume had made a quixotic attempt to succeed him that had been blocked by a campaign by the Kirk ministers.

Hume was content with Drs Black and Cullen, but was persuaded by Pringle to come to London for an examination, and then try the medicinal waters at Bath and Buxton. As it turned out, Smith had already set off, in company with the dramatist John Home, for Edinburgh. On 23 April, the two reached Morpeth in Northumberland, and, halting at the inn, saw Hume's servant, Colin Ross, lounging at the door. Smith was still keen to push on to Kirkcaldy to see his frail mother, while John Home would take the invalid south. That evening, they talked over Hume's literary posterity.

The problem was Hume's *Dialogues Concerning Natural Religion*, which had been circulating in Edinburgh since as early as 1750. The *Dialogues* hold scriptural religion up to critical examination and Hume had been dissuaded from publishing by friends such as Sir Gilbert Elliot and Hugh Blair. The prospect of his own extinction had rekindled Hume's interest. As literary executor, Smith wanted no part in publication. It was not that he thought the *Dialogues* were bad or boring. He later said they were 'finely written'.[5] He seems to have feared that association with the project might injure his chances of public employment. That evening in Morpeth, he referred to the scandal caused by the posthumous issue of the works of the controversial philosopher-politician Lord Bolingbroke by David Mallet in 1754.

Arrived in London, Hume wrote on 3 May: 'I think ... your scruples groundless. Was Mallet any wise hurt by the publication of Lord Bolingbroke? He received an office afterwards from the present King.'[6] None the less, he decided to leave the question of the *Dialogues* to Smith's discretion. In an 'ostensible' or formal letter he attached, Hume wrote: 'I have become sensible that, both on account of the nature of the work, and of your situation, it may be improper to hurry on that publication.'[7]

In a man who was not teaching young people, was well-off and had spoken of the sanctity of last wishes in the *Theory*, Smith's prudence seems excessive. The *Dialogues* were published by Hume's nephew to profound indifference. Smith had his reward when his own plans to immortalise his friend upset a clerical hornet's nest.

Smith whiled away the early summer, toying with a project that had occupied spare moments, probably since college days. Usually referred to as the 'Imitative Arts', this fragment examines a problem that has fascinated philosophers since Plato: why is it that a picture of a carpet should be more precious to a human being than the carpet itself? Smith stands by imitation as an aesthetic principle, but his interest is in what precisely is being imitated. The exact copy of a picture, painted statuary and *trompe l'oeil* effects are either wearisome or self-defeating, while music pleases by its 'great disparity' from the emotion it echoes. Hutcheson, it will be remembered, believed human beings were equipped with a sort of faculty that responded to beauty independent of will. Smith, in contrast, sees considerations of cost or fashion, of class allegiance or animosity, or love of system influence our reactions to a work of art. Seeing cut yew trees in the 'cabbage-garden of a tallow-chandler', the fashionable become disgusted even with Versailles.[8]

Smith was also fretting about the dismal performance of the British forces in America. Britain, it seems, though it abounded in great lawyers and watchmakers 'seems to breed neither statesmen nor generals'.[9] Hearing that the waters of Bath had disagreed with Hume, he wrote on 16 June with some proprietary diagnostics, recommending travel and a change of air: 'sauntering thro all the different corners of England' and then, in the autumn, 'visiting the venerable remains of ancient and modern arts that are to be seen about Rome and the Kingdom of Naples'.[10] This plan proved mere fancy when Hume arrived in Edinburgh on 3 July in 'a very shattered condition'. The next day, memorable for events across the Atlantic in Philadelphia, Hume received Smith and others of his Scots friends to dinner. Smith wrote to their publisher William Strahan, on 6 July, that his friend was 'by no means in the state in which I could have wished to have seen him. His spirits, however, continue perfectly good.'[11]

Adam Smith and David Hume believed that a man could be good without much or indeed any religious belief. For that to be demon-strated, it was necessary not only to live without fault but also to die without fear. As Hume put it to James Boswell, as he lay on a sofa in St David's Street on 7 July: 'If there were a future state, Mr Boswell, I think I could give as good an account of my life as most people.' Among the books he had with him that Sunday was *The Wealth of Nations*, 'which he commended much'.

Boswell, for whom the very notion of the virtuous infidel was a paradox, was overwhelmed with religious panic, scurrying for security to the half-remembered lectures of his mother and Dr Johnson.[12] So disturbed was the poor man that he would liquor himself up and, full to the brim with eternal truths, haunt the building sites round St David's Street. In one act of crapulous defiance, he picked up 'a big fat whore' and took her to a mason's shed beside Hume's house.[13]

In the middle of the month, Smith stayed with Hume at St David's Street. Confined to his room in the glorious hay-making weather, Hume told his friends that he was being shown by Smith how to enjoy it 'by Sympathy'. Likewise, a dinner he could not attend at stingy Adam Ferguson's.[14] But Smith felt obliged to leave when he saw that his company tired his friend. Back in Kirkcaldy on 14 August, he wrote to Alexander Wedderburn in London: 'Poor David Hume is dying very fast, but with great chearfulness and good humour and with more real resignation to the necessary course of things, than any whining Christian ever dyed with a pretended resignation to the will of God.' Like characters in his favourite classical author, Lucian, Hume imagined he was bargaining with the infernal boatman for some stay of execution. 'I began to think of what excuse I could alledge to Charon in order to procure a short delay, and as I have now done everything that I ever intended to do, I acknowledge for some time no tolerable one occurred to me; at last I thought I might say, Good Charon, I have been endeavoring to open the eyes of people; have a little patience only till I have the pleasure of seeing the churches shut up, and the clergy sent about their business; but Charon would reply, O you loitering rogue; that wont happen these two hundred years; do you fancy I will give you a lease for so long a time? Get into the boat this instant.'[15]

On 22 August, Smith wrote from Kirkcaldy asking Hume's permission to supplement 'My Own Life' with an account 'in my own name, of your behaviour in this illness, if, contrary to my own hopes, it should prove your last'.[16] His letter crossed with a bulletin from Dr Black, which described the invalid as 'much weaker' but still, at least, able to read.[17] On 23 August, still worrying at the question of the *Dialogues*, Hume dictated a last letter by the hand of his nephew. 'I go very fast to decline,' he wrote and signed it: 'Adieu My dearest Friend.'[18] Two days later, at 4 p.m. on Sunday afternoon, David Hume died. He died, said Joseph Black in a letter to Smith of the 26th, 'in such a happy composure of mind, that nothing could have made it better'.[19]

The account of Hume's last illness, one of the very finest pieces Smith ever wrote, occupied much of September, not just in the writing, but in the submission to Hume's friends, including Hume's older brother John, Black and John Home.[20] It was published in the form of a letter to his own and Hume's publisher William Strahan, and dated from Kirkcaldy on 9 November.

In the open letter to Strahan, Smith dropped the insulting phrase 'whining Christian' and replaced the Hume-English 'seeing the churches shut up' with the Smith-Latin 'seeing the downfal of some of the prevailing systems of superstition'. Smith's approach, which he no doubt thought prudent, was to turn Hume from an anti-Christian to a sort of ante-Christian: that is, to convert him from a modern sceptic into a philosopher of antique character. In the close, he reproduces the

Attic restraint of the obituary for Socrates with which Plato closes the *Phaedo*.[21] 'Upon the whole, I have always considered him, both in his lifetime and since his death, as approaching as nearly to the idea of a perfectly wise and virtuous man, as perhaps the nature of human frailty will permit.'[22]

The identification of Hume and Socrates compounded the great offence Smith had already caused, in his criticism of Oxford in *The Wealth of Nations*, to the circle of Dr Johnson and the English churchmen. The Revd George Horne, president of Magdalen College, Oxford, took the field against him. Horne's unsigned pamphlet, 'A Letter to Adam Smith, LL.D., on the Life, Death and Philosophy of David Hume, Esq. By one of the People called Christians', was widely read and is still easy to find. Both shrill and unctuous in tone, it is also abusive to both philosophers, and Smith was wise to ignore it. Boswell dropped him.[23] Smith seems to have been genuinely perplexed and later told Andreas Holt, a Danish customs official he had met in Toulouse: 'A single, and as, I thought a very harmless sheet of paper which I happened to write concerning the death of our late friend Mr Hume, brought upon me ten times more abuse than the very violent attack I had made upon the whole commercial system of Great Britain.'[24]

Whatever Smith's misgivings, the 'Letter' did not prevent preferment. In 1777, death created a vacancy among the five Commissioners of the Customs Board in Edinburgh, responsible for collecting duties on imported goods and for suppressing smuggling in Scotland. Though a Tory administration was now in power, Smith was well-connected. The Duchess of Buccleuch and Alexander Wedderburn, now Solicitor-General, wrote to support his cause with the Prime Minister, Lord

North. The Treasury secretary, Sir Grey Cooper, wrote to Smith in November teasing him for his diffidence in applying for so very insignificant a position.[25]

What was Adam Smith doing? His father, it will be remembered, had been a Customs man. Perhaps *The Wealth of Nations* had tired Smith out, and he had no wish to seclude himself again in Kirkcaldy for another decade with the Imitative Arts. A document, now at the University of Michigan, showed he was still active on American affairs after the crushing British defeat at Saratoga. Endorsed in the handwriting of Wedderburn, as 'Smith's Thoughts on the State of the Contest with America, February 1778', it was no doubt commissioned by him or by Henry Dundas, the administration's political manager in Scotland. (The memorandum repeats the liberal arguments of the *Wealth of Nations* for a federal union.) London, no doubt, beckoned but might be too much for his old mother. Gazetted as Commissioner in January 1778, Smith had second editions of the *The Wealth of Nations* 'handsomely bound and guilt' for both Cooper and Lord North.[26]

Smith was now as 'affluent as I could wish to be' on £900 a year, or more than the highest Scottish judges. He tried to give up the Buccleuch pension, but old pupil behaved to old governor in a way which was too exquisite even for *The Theory of Moral Sentiments*. In the set-piece biographical letter he wrote to Andreas Holt, Smith said: 'His Grace sent me word by his cashier, to whom I had offered to deliver up his bond, that though I had considered what was fit for my own honour, I had not consider'd what was fit for his; and that he never would suffer it to be suspected that he had procured an office for his friend, in order to deliver himself from the burden of such an annuity.'[27]

On receiving his commission, Smith moved his mother and Janet Douglas to Panmure House, a handsome, plain, old-fashioned L-shaped house with crow-stepped gabling that still stands in a close off the north side of the old aristocratic suburbs of Edinburgh, the Canongate. It had been the townhouse of a landed family that had forfeited its estates for taking part in the Jacobite rising of 1715. Hume had spent his last days amid the masons and building-sites of the New Town, but Smith's other friends such as Black, Hutton and Cullen had lingered in the old districts across the windy ravine. With its view of Calton Hill, Panmure House is as good a dwelling as any philosopher could wish. From it, Smith could walk the short mile up the High Street to the Custom-house, built by William Adam in the 1750s as the first of the civic improvements that were to make Edinburgh one of the finest towns in Europe. He could sit amid his sumptuous library – 'I am a beau in nothing but my books,' he once said[28] – and entertain his friends and philosophical visitors on Sunday nights in the thrifty and informal old Edinburgh style. At some point in 1778, this elderly household was joined by Smith's nine-year-old nephew, David Douglas, who was to become his heir.

For those who know Smith only by his reputation, it will be a surprise to find him a Commissioner of Customs, enforcing restrictions on the obvious system of natural liberty and pursuing smugglers at a time when 75 per cent of the trade in French goods was effectively prohibited. The surviving minutes of the Custom-house, studied by E. C. Mossner and I. S. Ross, show just how diligent Smith was in attending meetings in Edinburgh and signing letters to agents at the Scottish ports, or alerting ministers in London to the depredations of

Paul Jones and the American privateers.[29] Apart from visits to London in 1782 and 1787, Smith missed scarcely a meeting of the Commissioners and continued to attend even when he could no longer manage the walk up the High Street.

He had not altered his views on duties and prohibitions. In 1779, we find him urging British ministers to dismantle the 'unjust and oppressive restraints'[30] on imports from Ireland – mostly beef, glass and wool – banned or restrained under pressure from 'a very slender interest' of English manufacturers. As he wrote to Henry Dundas that November, 'Nothing, in my opinion, would be more highly advantageous to both countries than this mutual freedom of trade.'[31] In terms of the British revenue, he wrote in January 1780 to William Eden, an MP allied with Wedderburn who had interested himself in both America and Ireland, the 'sole effect of prohibition is to hinder the revenue from profiting by the importation', while 'high duties ... are equally hurtful to the revenue and equally favourable to smuggling, as absolute prohibitions'.[32] All the same, he believed in 'moderate and reasonable duties' on imported goods to defray the cost of the British administration in Scotland. 'The subjects of every state ought to contribute towards the support of the government.'[33] Smith saw the comedy in his situation. 'About a week after I was made a Commissioner of Customs,' he told Eden, 'upon looking over the list of prohibited goods (which is hung up in every Customhouse and which is well worth your considering) and upon examining my own wearing apparel, I found, to my great astonishment, that I had scarce a stock, a cravat, a pair of ruffles, or a pocket handkerchief which was not prohibited to be worn or used in Great Britain. I wished to set an example and burned them all. I will not advise you to examine your own or Mrs. Eden's apparel or household furniture, least you be brought into a scrape of the same kind.'[34]

Meanwhile, as the expenses of the American war multiplied and the prospect of victory became dim, Smith became more and more convinced, as he told the pioneering statistician John Sinclair of Ulster, of 'the real futility of all distant dominions ... which contribute nothing, either by revenue or military force, to the general defence of the empire'.[35] When Sinclair exclaimed that Britain must be ruined by the war, Smith replied, justly, 'Be assured, my young friend, that there is a great deal *of ruin* in a nation.'[36]

It is the Smith of these years that has become fixed in Edinburgh's long memory. As he walked up to the Custom-house, which still stands and now houses the Town Council, in the midst of the caddies and fish-wives, he was sketched by the barber turned caricaturist, John Kay. Smith is dressed smartly in coat, wig and hat, with a posy of flowers in his left hand (against the notorious stench of the High Street) and his cane over his shoulder. William Smellie, who was to print Robert Burns's poems from Anchor Close and edit and write most of the first *Encyclopaedia Britannica*, noted Smith carried his cane as a soldier does his musket.[37] (In June of 1781, Smith was made an honorary captain of the city guard. This was the so-called Trained Bands, generally made up of superannuated shopkeepers who, to impress their wives and mistresses, liked to discharge their weapons on parade. They had disgraced themselves in the 'Forty-five.[38]) As he walked, Smellie said, Smith's head had 'a gentle motion from side to side' and his body 'a kind of rolling or vermicular motion'.[39] The young Walter Scott, who was at the Edinburgh High School with David Douglas, was evidently taken to tea at Panmure House for he recalled Smith walking round and round, stopping every now and then to take a lump of sugar from the sugar-bowl, till Miss Douglas snatched it away and put it on her knee.[40] Scott later put it about that the marketwives of the Edinburgh High Street thought Adam was mad.[41]

As well as his 'Sunday night friends',[42] Smith instituted with Black and the geologist James Hutton a club called the 'Oyster Club', which met every Friday for dinner at a tavern in the Grassmarket. Since all three men were abstemious, meetings cannot have been absolutely riotous. Among those attending were a younger generation of Edinburgh savants such as the mathematician John Playfair, the moral philosopher Dugald Stewart and the geologist Sir James Hall. Among learned strangers, Barthélemy Faujas de Saint-Fond, a leading French vulcanologist, came to Edinburgh in the autumn of 1782 and saw a great deal of Smith.[43] They shared an admiration for both Rousseau and Voltaire.

One day Smith asked Saint-Fond if he liked music. The next day at nine o'clock, Smith came for his visitor and escorted him to a concert hall for the annual bag-pipe competition. A piper in Highland dress entered and began to play. Faujas found the noise excruciating, but Smith bade him listen carefully and then later describe the impression it made. If Smith was not teasing his guest, it does seem that he was continuing to work on his aesthetic theories – those sensations of 'colour, form, variety or rarity, and imitation'[44] – 'less,' as Dugald Stewart hurried to reassure everybody, 'with a view to the peculiar enjoyments they convey – than on account of their connexion with the general principles of the human mind; to an examination of which they afford the most pleasing of all avenues'.[45] For Faujas, there were few peculiar enjoyments from an instrument that 'lacerates the ear', but as he watched the 'beautiful Scottish ladies' weeping around him, he came to a conclusion that is highly Smithian: that the women's tears were aroused by an association of ideas, including the calamity of Scottish history.

Smith was one of the founder members, in 1783, of the Royal Society of Edinburgh. He used to join the geologist Hutton in his tramps up Arthur's Seat and to the Salisbury Crags. Smith seldom uttered a word but 'walked on moving his lips, and muttering to himself'.[46] Whether they conversed at all, Hutton's great *Theory of the Earth*, delivered on his behalf by Dr Black to the Royal Society of Edinburgh in early 1785, is a geological *Wealth of Nations* in which volcanoes and earthquakes are as integral to Nature's benign operations as the greed of merchants to those of society: 'useful for the safety of mankind, and as forming a natural ingredient in the constitution of the globe'.[47] There was, said Hutton, 'a circulation in the matter of this globe, and a system of beautiful oeconomy in the works of nature'.[48] Thus friendship has its consequences in different branches of science.

Henry Mackenzie, whose sentimental novel *The Man of Feeling* (1771) was a sort of *Theory of Moral Sentiments* gone weak at the knees, tried to have his hero contribute to his new sentimental periodical, *The Mirror*. Smith could never manage the sub-*Spectator* style and refused: 'My manner of writing,' he said, 'runs too much into deduction and inference.' Still, as a sort of elder statesman of literature, who had written for the first *Edinburgh Review* twenty-five years earlier, Smith was persuaded to criticise Mackenzie's two drafts for the farewell issue.[49]

In the spring of 1782, Smith had travelled to London to work on additions to *The Wealth of Nations* and to bring it abreast of the topical issues of the day, most notably the corruption and petty tyranny of the East India Company in its role in the government of India. He returned to Edinburgh in July. Progress was slow. On 7 December 1782, he wrote to Strahan's partner, Thomas Cadell, that the books he had brought up from London had 'debauched me from my proper business, the preparing a new edition of *The Wealth of Nations*'.[50] Dugald Stewart also blamed the Custom-house, for though his work there required no great mental effort from Smith, it was yet 'sufficient to waste his spirits and dissipate his attention'.[51]

Cadell, who liked to publish on topical subjects while Parliament was sitting, agreed to delay the additions to *The Wealth of Nations* to the following winter. In March 1783, Smith was promising Lady Frances Scott that he would revise his little paper on English and Italian verse (which survives), but was 'very much engaged in another business',[52] presumbly those changes. But in May, he was still waiting on information on the bounty systems from Sir Grey Cooper. Those had still not been sent by November. Smith had planned to make another trip to London, but, with his habitual kindness and providence, had given away his funds to a 'Welch nephew'.[53]

By the spring of 1784, he was correcting proofs but was delayed first by a visit from Edmund Burke, who had been appointed Lord Rector of Glasgow. They travelled to that city in April. Then, Smith suffered a reverse. His mother, Margaret Smith, always his closest attachment, died on 23 May. His letter to Strahan is unbearable. 'The death of a person in the ninetieth year of her age was no doubt an event most agreable to the course of nature; and, therefore, to be foreseen and prepared for; yet I must say to you, what I have said to other people, that the final separation from a person who certainly loved me more than any other person ever did or ever will love me; and whom I certainly loved and respected more than I ever shall either love or respect any other person, I cannot help feeling, even at this hour, as a very heavy stroke upon me.'[54]

The additions to *The Wealth of Nations* were finally published in November 1784. In the end, according to Smith's modern editors, they amounted to thirteen new sections and 24,000 words, including new arguments against the corn and herring bounties and in favour of trade with France.[55] The powerful account of the monopoly trading companies of the mercantile era, including the East India Company, was too late to help Burke's India Bill, which had foundered on party politics and the King's opposition earlier that year. Echoing the disgruntled Dutch India merchant, William Bolts, Smith pronounced that 'the government of an exclusive company of merchants is, perhaps, the worst of all governments for any country whatever.'[56] Still Henry Mackenzie, in his *Review of the Parliament of 1784*, credited Smith and his 'genius chastened by wisdom' with burying many old prejudices against trade with France.[57] The new government under William Pitt was, until war broke out again with France in the 1790s, more committed to free trade than any in British history.

Smith seems to have lost some of his spirit. He was now sixty-one, a good age for the eighteenth century. In the letter of 1785 to the duc de

La Rochefoucauld, mentioned earlier, Smith insisted he still had two great works 'upon the anvil': one the 'sort of philosophical history of all the different branches of literature, of philosophy, poetry and eloquence' and the other the 'sort of theory and history of law and government'. Yet, Smith was beginning to lose hope. 'The indolence of old age, tho' I struggle violently against it, I feel coming fast upon me, and whether I shall ever be able to finish either is extremely uncertain.'[58]

In the winter of 1786–7, Smith was laid low with chronic obstruction of the bowel. His plans to visit London for treatment must have been reinforced by a beguiling invitation from Henry Dundas, who now controlled patronage not only in Scotland but in India, and the Prime Minister. 'I am glad you have got vacation. Mr Pitt, Mr Greenville [i.e. William Grenville, later Prime Minister] and your humble servant are clearly of opinion you cannot spend it so well as here. The weather is fine, my villa at Wimbledon a most comfortable healthy place. You shall have a comfortable room and as the business is much relaxed we shall have time to discuss all your books with you every evening.'[59]

Smith was well enough to travel south, but acquaintances in London were shocked by his deterioration. He was treated for inflammation of the bladder and piles by John Hunter, the King's surgeon. John Kay's editor heard a story that one day at Dundas's house, when Smith was one of the last to enter the room, the Prime Minister, Grenville, the later Prime Minister Henry Addington, the anti-slavery campaigner William Wilberforce, and Dundas all stood up. 'We will stand till you are first seated,' Pitt said, 'for we are all your scholars.'[60] It sounds most unlikely. More characteristic was Wilberforce's account of Smith pouring cold water on a government scheme to bring employment to the Highlands. It is possible that it was during this visit that Smith sat for the only formal portrait done from life, a three-inch bust medallion in two states by the Scots modeller James Tassie, which is dated 1787. Both states show Smith in profile, one in modern dress and a bag wig, the other bare-shouldered and bare-headed in the antique manner. They can be seen in the Scottish National Portrait Gallery in Edinburgh.

Soon after his return to Scotland, Smith received an even more flattering invitation: to serve as Lord Rector of his *alma mater*, the University of Glasgow. In his reply to Principal Archibald Davidson, on 16 November, Smith displayed a certain emotion: 'No man can own greater obligations to a society than I do to the University of Glasgow – The period of thirteen years which I spent as a member of that society I remember as by far the most useful, and, therefore, as by the far the happiest and most honourable period of my life.'[61] At his installation in December, Smith seems to have remained quite silent, but at some point during the visit, he delivered to the town's Literary Society two lectures on the 'Imitative Arts'. These correspond to the two sections, on the plastic arts and on music, which were printed by Hutton and Black. There is also an unfinished third section on dancing.

By the spring of the new year, 1788, Smith was using his remaining strength to revise the *Theory*. On 15 March, he wrote to Thomas Cadell in London: 'As I consider my tenure of this life as extremely precarious, and am very uncertain whether I shall live to finish several other works which I have projected and in which I have made some progress, the best thing, I think, I can do is to leave those I have already published in the best and most perfect state behind me.' He went on to give a picture of his laborious way of writing. 'I am a slow a very slow workman, who do and undo everything I write at least half a dozen times before I can be tolerably pleased with it.'[62] He promised the revisions by June but could not keep the promise when Janet Douglas fell ill. She had been with Smith, apart from during his travels in England and France, since he had first set up house in Glasgow nearly forty years earlier. She had always been popular with his students for her 'humour and raillery'.[63]

By September, she had 'for some time' taken to her bed. On 16 September, Smith wrote to an old friend from Oxford, James Menteith, to thank him for a present of game, and added: 'Poor Miss Douglas … directs the affairs of the family, which she expects to leave in a few days, with as much care and distinctness as ever; and tho' sorry to part with her friends, seems to die with satisfaction and contentment, happy in the life that she has spent, and very well pleased with the lot that has fallen to her, and without the slightest fear or anxiety about the change she expects so soon to undergo.'[64] Smith found this philosophical tone hard to maintain, for six days later he wrote to his old pupil, Henry Herbert, Lord Porchester, who had been fond of her: 'She will leave me one of the most destitute and helpless men in Scotland.'[65]

Reading *The Wealth of Nations* in the west of Scotland in 1789, Robert Burns longed for a new edition that would present Smith's ideas on those countries, presumably France, America and India, 'that are or have been the scenes of considerable revolutions [i.e. developments] since his book was written'.[66] But as late as March 1789, Smith was still 'labouring very hard' on the additions to the *Theory*, including an entire new section, entitled 'Of the Character of Virtue', which amounted to a 'practical system of morality'. In fact, Smith wrote, 'I have even hurt my health', and returned to the Custom-house, 'princi-

pally for the sake of relaxation, and a much easier business'.[67] In a letter
to Dundas, he described his mind as 'melancholy and evil boding'.[68]

The young poet Samuel Rogers, who visited Smith in the summer,
found him excellent company, hospitable, kind and alert. Rogers arrived
in Edinburgh on the famous 14 July 1789, but there was no news of the
storming of the Bastille when he walked down the Canongate to call on
Smith the next morning. He found the philosopher sitting at breakfast,
quite alone, before a dish of strawberries. Smith, who was always kind
to young men, spoke in his usual forthright manner, and invited the
young visitor to the Oyster Club the next day, where the conversation
was unfortunately monopolised by a member named Ogle. On Sunday,
Rogers called on Smith as the bells were ringing for Kirk service. No
great churchgoer at the best of times, Smith was going out for an airing
in his sedan chair, but hospitably invited Rogers both to supper that
day and also to early afternoon dinner on Monday, when the 'Man of
Feeling' Henry Mackenzie was expected. After dinner, they proceeded
to a meeting of the Royal Society of Edinburgh to hear the political
economist James Anderson give a 'very long and dull' talk on the law
relating to debtors. 'Mr Commissioner Smith fell asleep,' Rogers
noted.[69] So much for the mature Smith's interest in economics. Finally,
on 18 November 1789, Smith wrote to Cadell that the revisions were
complete.[70]

What were these alterations that exhausted Smith's last thoughts?

On the debit side, he dropped the coupling of Mandeville with the
seventeenth-century duc de La Rochefoucauld. His friends, the present
duke and his mother, the duchesse d'Enville, had found it gratuitous
and offensive. The perverse result was to reveal to modern readers his

exclusive debt to the philosophical *roué* Mandeville. He also cut out a passage of conventional Presbyterian theology and high-flying rhetoric that must have survived as a sort of lump from his ethics lectures at Glasgow. His treatment of the Christian doctrine of atonement – that is, Christ's intercession for the sins of humanity – he replaced with a passage altogether more worldly and suave. 'In every religion, and in every superstition that the world has ever beheld,' he wrote, 'accordingly, there has been a Tartarus as well as an Elysium; a place provided for the punishment of the wicked, as well as one for the reward of the just.'[71]

On the credit side, the author of *The Wealth of Nations* had become less sanguine about the composition of social life based on possession and hierarchy. His experience of courts and drawing-rooms had, no doubt, shown him that wisdom and virtue had little chance against fashion and power. In a new chapter for Book One, he wrote that the 'disposition to admire, and almost to worship, the rich and the powerful', while to an extent natural and conducive to the peace of society, was 'at the same time the great and most universal cause of the corruption of our moral sentiments'.[72] We follow the fashions they set, including their fashionable vices. At the bottom and in the middle of society, where old Puritan values hold sway, the road to virtue often coincides with the road to worldly fortune. 'Real and solid professional abilities,' Smith writes, 'can very seldom fail of success.' But 'in the courts of princes, in the drawing-rooms of the great', success and preferments depend 'upon the fanciful and foolish favour of ignorant, presumptuous and proud superiors'. Solid virtues are 'held in the utmost contempt and derision'.[73]

The Impartial Spectator can adjust some of this distortion. The greatest benefit brought by wealth is not luxury but 'the respect of our equals'. It is the desire not just for this respect, but *actually to earn it*, 'of becoming the proper objects of this respect, of deserving and obtaining this credit and rank among our equals, is perhaps the strongest of all our desires'.[74] This, more than the isolated and systematical appetites of *The Wealth of Nations*, seem to be Smith's mature and considered thoughts on the sentiments that drive commercial society.

He then turns his attention to the new spirit of revolution in Europe and North America. In defining a political system as a complex of petty powers, privileges and immunities, Smith poses the dilemma of the 'real patriot' at times of radical change. 'It often requires, perhaps, the highest effort of political wisdom,' he writes, 'to determine when a real patriot ought to support and endeavour to re-establish the authority of the old system, and when he ought to give way to the more daring, but often dangerous spirit of innovation.' Smith had long recognised that men pursue systems, whether in cosmology or the arrangement of furniture, purely for the sake of system. In politics, this man of system – this Robespierre or Pol Pot – becomes so 'enamoured with the supposed beauty of his own ideal plan of government, that he cannot suffer the smallest deviation from any part of it ... He seems to imagine that he can arrange the different members of a great society with as much ease as the hand arranges the different pieces upon a chess-board.' Yet that risked transgressing what Smith calls the 'divine maxim of Plato, never to use violence to his country no more than to his parents'.[75] The maxim is put by Plato into the mouth of Socrates in prison, and shows that Smith was thinking about how philosophers die.

In this frame of mind, Smith addressed at last the capital source of both his philosophy and his sentiments, which was his orphan condition. For the first and last time in his writings, Smith uses the word 'fatherless'. While our good actions rarely have their effect much beyond our immediate circle, our goodwill can embrace the universe. Yet such universal benevolence will be productive only of misery and frustration unless we are convinced that an all-wise Being has ordered the universe for the best for all time. 'To this universal benevolence, on the contrary, the very suspicion of a fatherless world, must be the most melancholy of all reflections; from the thought that all the unknown regions of infinite and incomprehensible space may be filled with nothing but endless misery and wretchedness. All the splendour of the highest prosperity can never enlighten the gloom with which so dreadful an idea must necessarily overshadow the imagination.' In contrast, those who believe in the Stoical-Christian Providence that admits 'no partial evil which is not necessary for the universal good' will more readily resign themselves to their own and others' misfortunes. They are like good soldiers who are happy to march out on hopeless missions. Perhaps the wise man ought to consider that 'he himself, his friends and countrymen, have only been ordered upon the forlorn station of the universe'.

Here, if only for an instant, Smith seems to look up from his philosophical machines and out over the roofs. The metaphysical ghosts that Smith chased from his rooms back in his student days in Glasgow come crowding in. Maybe our responsibilities to creation go beyond sociability and free commerce? The moment passes. He returns to earth. All this universal benevolence, he writes, is the business of God, not man. Men should look for their own happiness, and that of their families and friends and country. What is the use of the sublime thoughts of the Roman Emperor Marcus Aurelius if you neglect the business of the Roman Empire?[76]

The revisions were printed early in 1790 and were the last of his writings published in his life. On 9 February, Smith excused himself from attending Dr Cullen's funeral because of a 'stomach complaint'.[77] He no longer had the strength to walk to the Custom-house. Twelve copies of the revised edition of the *Theory* arrived in May. Thanking Cadell on the 25th, he spoke of a planned trip to London, but he was so prone to 'violent relapses' that the journey 'becomes every day more doubtful'.[78]

That is the last of Smith's letters to survive. On 27 June, William Smellie wrote to Smith's friend Patrick Clason: 'Poor Smith! We must soon lose him; and the moment in which he departs will give a heart-felt pang to thousands. Mr Smith's spirits are flat; and I am afraid the exertions he sometimes makes to please his friends do him no good. His intellects, as well as his senses, are clear and distinct. He wishes to be cheerful; but nature is omnipotent. His body is extremely emaciated, because his stomach cannot admit of sufficient nourishment: but, like a man, he is perfectly patient and resigned.'[79]

As his end approached, Adam Smith began to fret about his surviving papers. He was not reassured by the promises of Hutton and Black that they would carry out his wishes and destroy them. Looking back on his life's work, Smith found his masterpieces paltry. He regretted 'he had done so little', said a witness to one of these mid-summer conversations. 'But I meant (said he) to have done more; and there are materials in my papers, of which I could have made a great deal. But that is now out of the question.'[80]

By Sunday, 11 July, Smith had become despondent. That day, according to Hutton, 'he begged one of them to destroy the volumes immediately. This accordingly was done.' What the volumes burned were we cannot know, but they were presumably not less than the eighteen volumes that Smith asked Hume back in 1773 to destroy 'without any examination'. Stewart believed that they included Smith's own notes to his lectures on rhetoric, natural religion and jurisprudence. What were left were some 'detached essays', comprising the 'Astronomy' and the other pieces that make up the *Essays on Philosophical Subjects* issued by Hutton, Black and Cadell's son, also Thomas, in 1795. As to why Smith undertook 'this irreparable injury to letters', Dugald Stewart assumed that he was dissatisfied with some of his arguments and did not wish to mislead the public.[81] Henry Mackenzie said there were sixteen volumes in manuscript which were 'the sum of one course of his lectures at Glasgow ...; but these had not received his last corrections and from what he had seen he had formed a mean opinion of posthumous publications in general.'[82] From those, it seems, Smith might have made his doomed philosophies of justice and taste. There may have been letters or verses to women. Whatever was in those folios, Hutton reported that Smith's 'mind was so much relieved that he was able to receive his friends in the evening with his usual complacency'.[83]

He retired before supper. As he left the room, he turned and, according to Henry Mackenzie, said: 'I love your company, gentlemen, but I believe I must leave you – to go to another world.'[84] Mackenzie, who tried to make a posthumous Christian out of David Hume, is less to be relied on than Hutton, who wrote: 'Mr Smith ... as he went away, took leave of his friends by saying, "I believe we must adjourn this meeting to some other place."'[85]

Smith died on Saturday, 17 July 1790. He was put in a corner of the Canongate churchyard, under a stone that states that the remains of Adam Smith, the author of *The Theory of Moral Sentiments* and *The Wealth of Nations*, are deposited there. The sympathetic visitor, though in the heart of a great capital city, looks up from Smith's tomb and sees lawns and woods, and arms of the sea, and distant mountains.

Notes

Introduction

1. 'Remarks by Chairman Alan Greenspan: *Adam Smith*, at the Adam Smith Memorial Lecture, Kirkcaldy, Scotland, February 6, 2005.' www.federalreserve.gov.
2. 'A sudden Blow from an almost invisible Hand, blasted all my Happiness.' Daniel Defoe, *The Fortunes and Misfortunes of the Famous Moll Flanders, etc.* (1722), London, 1989, p. 251.
3. *TMS*, p. 250.
4. *WN*, p. 613.
5. *WN*, p. 715.
6. Tyrants, *LJ*, p. 292. Madness: 'I remember Adam Smith's saying that half the people standing one day at the Cross of Edinburgh were mad without knowing it.' Henry Mackenzie, *Anecdotes and Egotisms*, ed. H. W. Thompson, Bristol, 1996, p. 173.
7. Monopolies, *WN*, p. 754; restraints on trade, p. 471; export subsidies, p. 874; and restrictions, p. 755; sumptuary laws, p. 872, *Corr*, p. 327; penal taxation, *WN*, p. 842; interest, p. 357; bank notes, p. 323; guild qualifications, p. 786; press,

Board of Customs Minutes, Vol. 16 in Ross, *Life*, p. 325; Roman Catholics, *LJ*, p. 299; nepotism, *Corr*, p. 185 etc.; public entertainment, *WN*, p. 796; federation, p. 944.

8. 'Adam Smith: Can Both the Left and Right Claim Adam Smith?' Edinburgh University, 25 April 2002. ed.ac.uk/events/lectures/enlightenment/adamsmith.html. 'The Hugo Young Memorial Lecture 2005: Full text of speech by Gordon Brown, Chancellor of the Exchequer, at Chatham House, London on December 13, 2005.' media.guardian. co.uk/presspublishing/comment/0,,1667303,00.

9. *TMS*, p. 234.

10. Hiroshi Mizuta, *Adam Smith's Library: A Catalogue*, Oxford, 2000.

11. Stockings, *WN*, p. 134; corn, *WN*, p. 461; 1,000-acre farm, Tom Teno, Centerville, Iowa, September 2004.

12. The notetaker wrote 100000, but the context shows he meant £100,000,000. *LJ*, p. 382.

13. *WN*, p. 32.

14. *WN*, p. 66.

15. *WN*, p. 85, p. 96, p. 795.

16. Thomas Malthus, *Essay on the Principle of Population*, London, 1798, p. 304.

17. *TMS*, p. 233.

18. To the Revd A. Alison, January 1793, in *Collected Works*, ed. Sir William Hamilton, Edinburgh, 1858, Vol. 10, p. 136.

19. *EPS*, p. 339.

20. Henry Cockburn, *Memorials of His Time*, Edinburgh, 1910, p. 41.
21. W. Smellie, *Literary and Characteristical Lives*, Edinburgh, 1800, p. 292.
22. Ramsay, *Scotland and Scotsmen*, Vol. 1, p. 468.
23. *TMS*, p. 299.
24. John Stuart Mill, 'On the Definition of Political Economy', in *Essays on Some Unsettled Questions of Political Economy*, London, 1864, p. 137.
25. John Stuart Mill, *Principles of Political Economy*, London, 1848, p. v.
26. He said General Williams of Kars. Karl Marx, *Capital* (1867), Vol. 1, New York, 1967, p. 125n.
27. Walter Bagehot, *Biographical Studies*, ed. R. H. Hutton, London, 1881, p. 273.

1 Fatherless World

1. To Andreas Holt, Edinburgh, 26 October 1780, in *Corr*, p. 252.
2. Potatoes, *WN*, p. 177; African, 'Imitative Arts', *EPS*, p. 209; jewels, 'Imitative Arts', *EPS*, p. 183; mariner, 'External Senses', *EPS*, p. 152; greyhounds, *WN*, p. 25; quack, To William Cullen, 20 September 1774, *Corr*, p. 176; slack-rope, *TMS*, p. 10; dyers, 'Astronomy', *EPS*, p. 44; pins, *WN*, p. 15; factory machines, *LJ*, p. 351; yews, 'Imitative Arts', *EPS*, p. 184; camp, *WN*, p. 97; beggars, *TMS*, p. 185.

3. 'It is certainly very remarkable that Adam Smith should have been a recluse student, during his whole life almost exclusively with abstractions, and that Ricardo, who is so eminently an abstract thinker, should have been bred up in actual business, and should have attained his powers of deductive reasoning without any early philosophical discipline. It would certainly have been expected, if we had not known how little outward circumstances avail against the intrinsic aptitudes of a strong mind, that Adam Smith would have looked on nature principally "through the spectacles of books," and that Ricardo would have taken that general, vague, but in the main sufficient, judgment upon matters of fact which is generally called "common sense," and which alone among the higher intellectual gifts is habitually exercised in every-day practical life.' Walter Bagehot, 'Review of Mill's *Principles of Political Economy*', *The Prospective Review*, Vol. IV, 16, 1848, p. 462.
4. *WN*, p. 898.
5. *WN*, p. 944.
6. To William Strahan, Glasgow, 4 April 1760, *Corr*, p. 68.
7. Daniel Defoe, *A Tour thro' the Whole Island of Great Britain divided into Circuits or Journies*, Vol. 4, London, 1753, p. 163.
8. Stewart, 'Life of Smith', *EPS*, p. 333.
9. *WN*, p. 18, p. 38.
10. 'External Senses', *EPS*, pp. 161ff.
11. Which is twice more than Plato.
12. 'External Senses', *EPS*, p. 152; *TMS*, p. 135; *WN*, p. 157.
13. Stewart, 'Life of Smith', *EPS*, p. 269.

14. Rae, *Life*, pp. 4–5. *TMS*, p. 210 has strikingly similar language and the story may, in reality, be a back-formation from that passage.

15. Stewart, 'Life of Smith,' *EPS*, p. 270.

16. Rae, *Life*, p. 5.

17. *WN*, p. 785.

18. *TMS*, p. 222.

19. *WN*, p. 764.

20. Defoe, *Tour*, Vol. 4, p. 122.

21. 'Il faut payer à nos voisins quatre millions d'un article et cinq ou six d'un autre, pour mettre dans notre nez une poudre puante, venue de l'Amérique.' Voltaire, *L'Homme aux 40 écus*, 1768, p. 2.

22. *WN*, pp. 372–3. J. Gibson, *History of Glasgow*, 1777, says 44 million out of 46 million pounds of tobacco imported into Glasgow were re-exported, pp. 213–34.

23. Stewart, 'Life of Smith', *EPS*, p. 330.

24. John Chamberlayne, *Magnae Britanniae Notitia*, London, 1737, Vol. 2, Bk. 3, pp. 12–13.

25. William Leechman, Preface, in Hutcheson's *System of Moral Philosophy*, p. xiii.

26. *WN*, p. 771.

27. *LJ*, p. 488.

28. *An Inquiry into the Original of our Ideas of Beauty and Virtue; in Two Treatises. In which the Principles of the late Earl of Shaftesbury are explain'd and defended, against the Author of the Fable of the Bees*, London, 1725.

29. *The Meditations of the Emperor Marcus Aurelius*, trans. Francis Hutcheson, Glasgow, 1742.

30. *TMS*, pp. 36, 289.

31. Hugo Grotius, 'To the Rulers and Free Peoples of Christendom', *Mare Liberum*, 1608/9. Carmichael edited a new version of Pufendorf's *De Officio Hominis et Civis* in 1724.

32. Hutcheson, *System*, Vol. 1, p. 294.

33. Hutcheson, *Short Introduction*, Bk 2; *System*, Vol. 1, pp. 288, 317; Vol. 2, pp. 53, 64.

34. Stewart, 'Life of Smith', *EPS*, p. 314.

35. To Dr Archibald Davidson, Edinburgh, 16 November 1787, *Corr*, p. 309.

36. Stewart, 'Life of Smith', *EPS*, p. 271.

37. *TMS*, p. 124.

38. H. W. Davis, *A History of Balliol College*, Oxford, 1963, p. 150.

39. *Corr*, p. 1.

40. *WN*, p. 772.

41. To Lord Shelburne, Glasgow, 31 August 1759, *Corr*, p. 45.

42. *Corr*, p. 3.

43. ibid.

44. Stewart, 'Life of Smith', *EPS*, p. 271.

45. ibid.

46. John Ramsay of Ochtertyre says Smith wrote and spoke English 'with great purity'. *Scotland and Scotsmen*, Vol. 1, p. 461.

47. To David Hume, Edinburgh, 16 April 1773, *Corr*, p. 168. W. P. D. Wightman lays out the arguments as to dating in his introduction to *EPS*, pp. 7–9.

48. To le duc de La Rochefoucauld, Edinburgh, 1 November 1785, *Corr*, pp. 286–7.

49. ibid.

50. To William Cullen, 29 September 1774, *Corr*, p. 177.

51. 'Astronomy', *EPS*, p. 46.

52. 'Astronomy', *EPS*, pp. 45–6.

53. 'Astronomy', *EPS*, p. 105.

54. Compare Immanuel Kant in his *Critique of Pure Reason* (1781) (ed. N. Kemp-Smith, 1965, pp. 147–8). 'The order and regularity in the appearances, which we entitle nature, we ourselves introduce. We could never find them in appearances, had not we ourselves, or the nature of our mind, originally set them there.'

55. 'Note by the Editors', *EPS*, p. 105.

56. 'Ancient Physics', *EPS*, p. 107.

57. Technology, *LJ*, p. 574; law, *LJ*, p. 42; politics, *TMS*, p. 232; topiary, 'Imitative Arts', *EPS*, pp. 183–4; chairs and toys, *TMS*, p. 180.

58. *LRBL*, p. 146. In *The Wealth of Nations*, Smith speaks of Greek science and ethics showing 'the beauty of a systematical arrangement of different observations connected by a few common principles'. *WN*, p. 768.

59. 'Ancient Physics', *EPS*, p. 111.

60. William Leechman, in his preface to Hutcheson's *System* in 1755, spoke of how 'the silent and unseen hand of an all-wise Providence' brought Hutcheson to the Glasgow moral philosophy chair, 'a station in life, which ... was perhaps of all others the most suited to the singular talents with which he was endowed, and gave him the opportunity of being more eminently and extensively useful than he could have been in any other'. Smith usually prefers a Latin derivation ('invisible') to an Anglo-Saxon ('unseen'). Hutcheson, *System*, p. xii.

61. 'Astronomy', *EPS*, p. 49.

2 Cave, Tree, Fountain

1. Stewart, 'Life of Smith,' *EPS*, p. 272.

2. Rae, *Life*, p. 30.

3. ''Tis done, my sons! 'Tis nobly done! / Victorious over tyrant power: / How quick the race of fame was won! / The work of ages in one hour.' 'Gladsmuir', in James Hogg, *Jacobite Relics*, 2nd series, Edinburgh, 1819–21, p. 119.

4. Alexander Fraser Tytler (Lord Woodhouselee), *Memoirs of the Life and Writings of the Honourable Henry Home of Kames*, Edinburgh, 1807, Vol. 2, Appendix 3.

5. His 'education' of Kattie Gordon is recorded in his letters in the Stewart of Afton Papers, BL. Add. 40635, fol. 27ff.

6. Hume to Smith, 8 June 1758, *Corr*, p. 24. John Chamberlayne, *Magnae Britanniae Notitia*, London, 1737, p. 443.

7. The first lecture of the Glasgow series is missing while the third, 'Of the Origin and Progress of Language', had been

published separately in 1761 as 'Considerations Concerning the First Formation of Languages', *The Philological Miscellany*, pp. 440–79.

8. *TMS*, p. 336.

9. *LRBL*, pp. 25–6.

10. Lord Monboddo, *Of the Origin and Progress of Language*, Edinburgh, 1773, pp. 174–5.

11. To George Baird, Glasgow, 7 February 1763, *Corr*, pp. 87–8. John Millar reported that Smith believed the best method of 'explaining and illustrating the various powers of the human mind, the most useful part of metaphysics, arises from the several ways of communicating our thoughts by speech, and from an attention to the principles of those literary compositions which contribute to persuasion or entertainment'. Stewart, 'Life of Smith', EPS, p. 274.

12. 'A Dictionary of the English Language by Samuel Johnson', *EPS*, p. 232.

13. *LRBL*, p. 112.

14. *LRBL*, p. 137.

15. *LJ*, p. 352.

16. *LRBL*, pp. 145–6.

17. Stewart, 'Life of Smith', *EPS*, p. 292.

18. Stewart, 'Life of Smith', *EPS*, p. 293.

19. Walter Bagehot, *Biographical Studies*, ed. R. H. Hutton, London, 1881, p. 255.

20. Stewart, 'Life of Smith', *EPS*, p. 293.

21. 'He who thus considers things in their first growth and origin, whether a state or anything else, will obtain the clearest view of them.' *Politica*, 1252a. Tacitus, *Annals*, 3, 26 'Vetustissimi mortalium ...' and *Germania*, throughout.
22. Stewart, 'Life of Smith', *EPS*, p. 296.
23. *LRBL*, p. 9.
24. *EPS*, pp. 187–8.
25. *EPS*, pp. 106–7.
26. *WN*, p. 25.
27. John Stuart Mill, 'On the Definition of Political Economy', in *Essays on Some Unsettled Questions of Political Economy*, London, 1864, p. 122.
28. 'A Letter from Governor Pownall to Adam Smith, LLD, FRS', 25 September 1776, *Corr*, p. 369.
29. 'Early Draft of Part of *The Wealth of Nations*', *LJ*, p. 573.
30. Hume, 'My Own Life', p. 4. The phrase is from Alexander Pope: 'All, all but Truth, drops dead-born from the Press, / Like the last Gazette, or the last Address.' Pope, *Epilogue to the Satires, Dialogue II*, ll. 226–7.
31. To William Cullen, Edinburgh, 3 September 1751, *Corr*, p. 5.
32. Stewart, 'Life of Smith', *EPS*, pp. 273–4.
33. *Corr*, p. 5.
34. 24 September 1752, *Corr*, p. 8.
35. To Dr Archibald Davidson, Edinburgh, 16 November 1787, *Corr*, p. 309.
36. *Corr*, p. 16.
37. Rae, *Life*, p. 69.

38. *TMS*, p. 237.
39. 'Reminiscences of James Watt', *Transactions of the Glasgow Archaeological Society*, 1859.
40. Scott, *Student and Professor*, p. 149.
41. 'Early Draft', *LJ*, p. 570.
42. *WN*, p. 20.
43. To William Strahan, Edinburgh, 26 October 1780, *Corr*, p. 248.
44. *WN*, p. 297.
45. Carlyle, *Autobiography*, pp. 81–2.
46. Ramsay, *Scotland and Scotsmen*, Vol. 1, p. 463.
47. A fragment on justice and punishment, now in Glasgow University Library, may be from the ethics lectures. It is printed at *TMS*, pp. 388–90. In addition, in the finished *Theory* there are inadvertent relics of lecture speech, such as 'as I observed on a former occasion'. *TMS*, pp. 189, 190, 316.
48. Stewart, 'Life of Smith', *EPS*, pp. 274–5.
49. Rae, *Life*, p. 59.
50. 'Every thing relative to so great a man is worth observing. I remember Dr Adam Smith, in his rhetorical lectures at Glasgow, told us he was glad to know that Milton wore latchets in his shoes, instead of buckles.' *The Journal of a Tour to the Hebrides* (1786) in Samuel Johnson and James Boswell, *A Journey to the Western Islands of Scotland and The Journal of a Tour to the Hebrides*, London, 1984, p. 165.
51. *Boswell: The Ominous Years, 1774–1776*, C. Ryskamp and F. A. Pottle (eds), London, 1963, p. 115.

52. To Lord Shelburne, Glasgow, 10 March 1759, *Corr*, p. 28; 4 April 1759, *Corr*, p. 31; 29 October 1759, *Corr*, p. 59. Oeconomy: From Lord Shelburne, Dublin, 26 April 1759, *Corr*, p. 37.

53. To Shelburne, 31 August 1759, *Corr*, p. 45.

54. 'Your presence dissipated in six months time much stronger prejudices in Edinburgh.' Smith to Hume, possibly Toulouse in September 1765, *Corr*, p. 108.

55. *WN*, p. 810.

56. *WN*, p. 796.

57. Scott, *Student and Professor*, pp. 164–5.

58. 'A Dictionary of the English Language by Samuel Johnson', in *EPS*, p. 232.

59. 'Letter to the *Edinburgh Review*', *EPS*, p. 253.

60. *TMS*, p. 234.

61. Stewart, 'Life of Smith', *EPS*, p. 321.

62. Stewart, 'Life of Smith', *EPS*, p. 322.

63. Hume to Allan Ramsay, April or May 1755. Hume, *Letters*, Vol. 1, pp. 220–21.

64. David Hume, *Political Essays*, ed. K. Haakonssen, Cambridge, 1996, p. 107.

65. Carlyle, *Autobiography*, p. 293.

3 Pen-knives and Snuff-boxes

1. Pen-knives and snuff-boxes, p. 94; tweezer-case, p. 181; ear-picker and nail-cutter, p. 182; chest, p. 188; button, p. 194; roads and servants, p. 42; joke, p. 14; aldermen's wives, p. 57.

2. Proud, vain, *TMS*, p. 255; liar, coxcomb, p. 115; nothing right, p. 42.
3. *LRBL*, p. 112.
4. *Corr*, pp. 34–5.
5. Edmund Burke, *Annual Register*, 1759, p. 485.
6. *Corr*, p. 46.
7. *TMS*, p. 265.
8. Hume, *Treatise*, p. 668.
9. *TMS*, p. 9.
10. *TMS*, p. 25.
11. και ψυχη ει μελλει γνωσεσθαι αυτην εις ψυχην αυτη βλεπτεον. Plato, *Alcibiades*, 133B.
12. *TMS*, p. 9.
13. *TMS*, p. 10.
14. Ibid.
15. *TMS*, p. 26.
16. *TMS*, p. 32.
17. *TMS*, p. 31.
18. *TMS*, p. 42.
19. *TMS*, p. 112.
20. 'Imitative Arts', *EPS*, p. 186. 'In a clown [i.e. rustic], who had never beheld a looking-glass before, I have seen that wonder rise almost to rapture and extasy.'
21. *TMS*, p. 130.
22. *TMS*, p. 242.
23. *TMS*, p. 326.

24. Francis Hutcheson, *An Inquiry Concerning the Original of our Ideas of Virtue or Moral Good*, 1725, Section 6; Ferguson, *Civil Society*, pp. 191–3; John Millar, 'Of the Rank and Condition of Women in Different Ages', *Origin of the Distinction of Ranks*, Edinburgh, 1771; Robert Burns, for example 'Green Grow the Rashes', 1783.

25. *TMS*, pp. 190–91.

26. *TMS*, p. 205.

27. Mary Wollstonecraft, *A Vindication of the Rights of Woman* (1792), London, 1992, pp. 149ff.

28. *TMS*, p. 135.

29. To Sir Gilbert Elliot, 10 October 1759, *Corr*, p. 49.

30. *TMS*, pp. 130–31.

31. *TMS*, p. 247.

32. Infant exposure, *TMS*, p. 210; boarding school, p. 222; Grand Tour, *WN*, p. 773.

33. *TMS*, p. 181.

34. *TMS*, pp. 182–3.

35. *TMS*, p. 183.

36. *TMS*, p. 253.

37. *TMS*, p. 226.

38. *TMS*, p. 86.

39. Steuart, *Inquiry*, p. 281.

40. Marquis de Mirabeau, *Philosophie rurale*, Paris, 1764, Vol. 1, p. 117.

41. *TMS*, pp. 184–5.

42. *TMS*, pp. 59n., 105, 128 and n., 170, 236, 277–8, 290, 292 etc.
43. *TMS*, p. 185.

4 Infidel with a Bag Wig

1. *TMS*, pp. 341–2.
2. *LRBL*, p. 25.
3. *TMS*, p. 3.
4. *Corr*, p. 168.
5. E. Cannan (ed.), *Lectures on Justice, Police, Revenue and Arms delivered in the University of Glasgow by Adam Smith*, Oxford, 1896.
6. University of Strathclyde, Anderson Library, MS 35.1.
   R. L Meek, 'New Light on Adam Smith's Glasgow Lectures on Jurisprudence', *History of Political Economy*, Vol. 8, 1976.
7. *TMS*, p. 389.
8. *LJ*, pp. 17, 18, 19, 32, 87, 104, 459, 461, 475.
9. *TMS*, p. 389.
10. Scott, *Student and Professor*, p. 318.
11. *LJ*, pp. 582–6.
12. *Corr*, p. 36.
13. *Corr*, p. 48.
14. *Corr*, p. 58.
15. *Corr*, p. 95.
16. *WN*, p. 774.
17. *Corr*, p. 36.
18. Rae, *Life*, p. 153.

19. 'I can never forget, that it is the very same species, that wou'd scarce show me common civilities a very few years ago at Edinburgh, who now receive me with such applauses at Paris.' *Corr*, p. 97.

20. *Corr*, p. 414.

21. *LJ*, p. 483. Thomas Pennant, *A Tour in Scotland in 1769*, Warrington, 1774, p. 58.

22. Alexander Fraser Tytler (Lord Woodhouselee), *Memoirs of the Life and Writings of The Honourable Henry Home of Kames*, Edinburgh, 1807, Vol. 1, p. 195.

23. From Joseph Black, Glasgow, 23 January 1764, *Corr*, p. 99.

24. *TMS*, p. 120. Did Smith know the poem Montrose wrote in the Edinburgh Tolbooth on the night before his execution, 20–21 May 1650? 'Let them bestow on every airth a limb, / Then open all my veins, that I may swim / To Thee, my Maker, in that crimson lake.' Voltaire quotes these lines in his *Essai sur l'histoire générale*.

25. *Corr*, p. 101.

26. 'Il parlait fort mal notre langue.' *Mémoires de l'Abbé Morellet*, Paris, 1821, Vol. 1, p. 237.

27. *Corr*, p. 102.

28. To David Hume, Toulouse, 21 October 1764, *Corr*, p. 102.

29. *Corr*, p. 103.

30. *Corr*, p. 104.

31. *TMS*, p. 54.

32. *Corr*, p. 109.

33. *TMS*, pp. 214–15.

34. 'From Madam d'Anville ... he received many attentions, which he always recollected with particular gratitude.' Stewart, 'Life of Smith', *EPS*, p. 303.

35. *TMS*, pp. 308–9.

36. *Corr*, p. 108.

37. *Corr*, p. 110.

38. To comtesse de Boufflers, 15 July 1766, Hume, *Letters*, Vol. 2, p. 63.

39. It is signed 'Le Gr Vic Ecossois', which might be the Abbé Colbert. *Corr*, p. 111.

40. Dugald Stewart wrote in 1811 that 'in the early part of Mr Smith's life it is well known to his friends, that he was for several years attached to a young lady of great beauty and accomplishment. How far his addresses were favourably received, or what the circumstances were which prevented their union, I have not been able to learn; but I believe it is pretty certain that, after this disappointment, he laid aside all thoughts of marriage. The lady to whom I allude died also unmarried. She survived Mr Smith for a considerable number of years ... I had the pleasure of seeing her when she was turned of eighty, and when she still retained evident traces of her former beauty.' 'Life of Smith', *EPS*, pp. 349–50.

41. Stewart, 'Life of Smith', *EPS*, p. 305.

42. To R. Liston, 21 May 1766; to D. Garrick, October 1766. J. C. Nicholls, 'Mme Riccoboni's Letters to David Hume, David Garrick, and Sir Robert Liston, 1764–1783', *Studies*

on *Voltaire and the Eighteenth Century*, 149, Oxford, 1976, pp. 71, 88–9, 100.

43. Charles Augustin Sainte-Beuve, *Nouveaux Lundis*, Paris, 1863–72, Vol. 8, pp. 346–7.

44. Lettre 97, *Lettres de Mistriss Fanni Butlerd à Milord Charles Alfred, duc de Caitonbridge*, Paris, 1757.

45. *Mémoires de Morellet*, Vol. 1, p. 237.

46. *Quesnay's Tableau économique*, ed. M. Kuczynski and R. L. Meek, London, 1972.

47. Marquis de Mirabeau, *Philosophie rurale*, Amsterdam, 1763, Vol. 1, pp. 52–3; quoted in *WN*, p. 679.

48. *WN*, p. 674.

49. *WN*, p. 663.

50. *Corr*, pp. 115–16.

51. Rae, *Life*, p. 226.

52. *Corr*, p. 120.

53. *Corr*, p. 121.

54. Rae, *Life*, p. 226.

55. *Corr*, p. 121.

56. Carlyle, *Autobiography*, p. 294.

57. *TMS*, p. 152.

58. Stewart, 'Life of Smith', *EPS*, p. 306.

59. Scott, *Scotland and Scotsmen*, Vol. 1, p. 464.

60. *Corr*, p. 123.

61. Adam Anderson, *An historical and chronological deduction of the Origin of Commerce*, London, 1764.

62. To Thomas Cadell, 25 March 1766 (i.e. 1767), *Corr*, p. 124.

63. *Corr*, p. 125.
64. To John Craigie, Kirkcaldy, 26 June 1767, *Corr*, p. 130.
65. Carlyle, *Autobiography*, p. 512.
66. To Andreas Holt, Edinburgh, 26 October 1780, *Corr*, p. 252.
67. 27 January 1768, *Corr*, pp. 137–8.
68. *Corr*, p. 140.
69. 20 August 1769, *Corr*, p. 155.
70. The letter is undated, possibly 1771. *Corr*, p. 160.
71. Robert Chambers, *A Picture of Scotland*, Edinburgh, 1827, p. 220.
72. Sir William Forbes, *Memoirs of a Banking-house*, Edinburgh, 1860, p. 39.
73. *Corr*, p. 162.
74. Kirkcaldy, 3 September 1772, *Corr*, p. 163.
75. *The precipitation and fall of Mess. Douglas, Heron, and Company, late Bankers in Air, with the causes of their ... ruin, investigated ... by a Committee of Inquiry, appointed by the proprietors*, Edinburgh, 1778.
76. *Corr*, p. 164.
77. *Corr*, p. 415.
78. *Corr*, p. 168.
79. Kames to Daniel Fellenberg, 20 April 1773, MS, Bürgerbibliothek, Berne, Switzerland, in Ross, *Life*, p. 245.
80. *Corr*, p. 168.
81. *Corr*, p. 252.
82. Mossner, *Life of Hume*, p. 554.
83. *WN*, pp. 625–6.

84. *Corr*, pp. 173–9.
85. C. Ryskamp and F. A. Pottle (eds.), *Boswell: The Ominous Years, 1774–1776*, London, 1963, p. 337.
86. *Corr*, p. 182.
87. Bowness, 1 November 1775, *Corr*, p. 184.
88. Edinburgh, 8 February 1776, *Corr*, p. 185.
89. Henry Thomas Buckle, *History of Civilization in England*, London, 1857–61, Vol. 1, p. 194 .

5 Baboons in the Orchard

1. 'Le Mondain', 1736.
2. *LJ*, p. 335.
3. *WN*, p. 181.
4. Mandeville, *Fable*, Vol. 1, pp. 355–6.
5. David Hume, *Political Essays*, ed. K. Haakonssen, Cambridge, 1996, p. 107.
6. Steuart, *Inquiry*, p. 44.
7. *WN*, p. 456.
8. *LJ*, p. 343.
9. In fact, Mandeville describes honest women as 'uncomatable'. *Fable*, Vol. 1, p. 95.
10. *LJ*, p. 390.
11. *LJ*, pp. 486, 398.
12. *WN*, p. 428.
13. 'Il n'en coûte guères plus aujourd'hui pour être agréablement logé, qu'il en coûtait pour l'être mal sous *Henri IV*.' Voltaire, *Siècle de Louis XIV*, Geneva, 1768, Vol. 3, p. 54.

14. *LJ*, p. 341.
15. Mandeville, *Fable*, Vol. 1, pp. 169–70.
16. Plato, *Symposium*, 221.
17. *WN*, p. 15.
18. Sir William Petty, 'Political Arithmetick' (1690), *The Economic Writings of Sir William Petty*, New York, 1963, Vol. 1, p. 260.
19. Mandeville, *Fable*, Vol. 2, pp. 141–2.
20. Hume, *Treatise*, p. 537.
21. Plato, *Republic*, 370.
22. *LJ*, p. 196.
23. *WN*, p. 28.
24. *WN*, p. 25.
25. *LJ*, p. 352.
26. Ibid.
27. John Stuart Mill, 'On the Definition of Political Economy', in *Essays on Some Unsettled Questions of Political Economy*, London, 1864, p. 122.
28. *WN*, pp. 26–7.
29. *TMS*, p. 86.
30. *WN*, p. 45.
31. *WN*, p. 66.
32. *WN*, p. 67.
33. *WN*, p. 68.
34. *WN*, p. 265.
35. *WN*, p. 75.
36. *WN*, p. 73.
37. *WN*, p. 138.

38. *WN*, p. 96.

39. *WN*, p. 145.

40. *WN*, p. 163.

41. *WN*, p. 267.

42. *WN*, p. 287.

43. *WN*, p. 282.

44. *WN*, p. 284.

45. *WN*, p. 321.

46. *WN*, p. 331.

47. 'Imitative Arts', *EPS*, p. 187.

48. *WN*, p. 796.

49. *WN*, p. 330.

50. Adam Smith, 'Of Luxury', in *Political Discourses*, 1752; 'Of Refinement in the Arts', in *Essays and Treatises on Several Subjects*, 1758.

51. *WN*, pp. 341, 343.

52. *WN*, p. 345.

53. *WN*, pp. 16–17.

54. *WN*, p. 378.

55. *WN*, p. 385.

56. *WN*, p. 405.

57. *WN*, p. 471.

58. *WN*, p. 456.

59. Ferguson, *Civil Society*, pp. 119–20.

60. To de la Chalotais, *Voltaire's Correspondence*, 11 July 1762, *Oeuvres complètes*, ed. T. Besterman, Geneva, 1959, p.100.

61. *WN*, pp. 629–30. See also pp. 422 and 802–3, where the argument follows a similar cast, without the use of any hands, visible or invisible.

62. *WN*, p. 582.

63. *WN*, p. 625.

64. To Andreas Holt, Edinburgh, 26 October 1780, *Corr*, p. 251.

65. *WN*, p. 687.

66. *WN*, p. 428.

67. *WN*, p. 701.

68. *WN*, p. 715.

69. Henry Cockburn, *Memorials of His Time*, Edinburgh, 1910, p. 41.

70. *WN*, p. 725.

71. *WN*, p. 719.

72. *WN*, p. 788.

73. *LJ*, p. 539.

74. *WN*, pp. 786, 796.

75. *WN*, p. 761.

76. *WN*, p. 781.

77. A. Law, *Education in Edinburgh in the Eighteenth Century*, London, 1965, pp. 185–6. For labourers' wages in and about Edinburgh, *WN*, p. 94.

78. *WN*, p. 857.

79. *WN*, pp. 825–6.

80. Land, *WN*, pp. 831 and 844; ale-shops, p. 853; liquor, p. 891; luxuries, p. 872 and *Corr*, p. 327; coal, *WN*, p. 874; rich, p. 842; monopolists, p. 893.

81. *WN*, p. 870. Also, a student's 'necessary' and 'unnecessary' expenses at Glasgow, *Corr*, p. 41.

82. *WN*, pp. 928–9.

83. *WN*, p. 947.

84. *Corr*, p. 186.

85. *Corr*, pp. 187–9.

86. *Corr*, p. 190.

87. North Murchiston, 8 April 1776, *Corr*, p. 192.

88. Edinburgh, 18 April 1776, *Corr*, pp. 193–4.

89. C. McC. Weis and F. A. Pottle (eds.), *Boswell in Extremes, 1776–1778*, London, 1971, p. 210.

90. Carlyle, *Autobiography*, p. 295.

91. 'Governor Pownall's Letter', *Corr*, p. 337.

92. Edmund Burke, *Annual Register*, 1776, p. 241.

93. Steuart's was an 'attempt towards reducing to principles, and forming into a regular science, the complicated interests of domestic policy'. *Inquiry*, Preface.

94. Karl Marx, *A Contribution to the Critique of Political Economy* (1859), Note C, 'Theories of the Medium and Circulation of Money'.

95. Steuart, *Inquiry*, p. lv.

96. 'Esta reflexión [i.e. perfect liberty] puede ser exacta en un país ilustrado en que los particulares por lo general conozcan el uso mas ventajoso que pueden hacer de su dinero; pero hay otros en que los capitalistas necesitan que el Gobierno los lleve, por decirlo así, de la mano para que den movimiento a sus fondos, y los emplean con utilidad.' *Compendio de la obra intitulada*

Riqueza de las Naciones, hecho por el Marqués de Condorcet,
C. M. de Irujo, Madrid, 1792, p. 169n.

97. To Robert Graham, Ellisland, 13 May 1789, *Letters of Robert Burns*, ed. J. Ferguson, Oxford, 1931, Vol. 1, p. 335.

98. *LJ*, pp. 347, 492–3, 570, 574.

99. *WN*, p. 341.

100. *LJ*, p. 42.

101. *WN*, p. 440.

102. *LJ*, p. 262.

103. *WN*, pp. 418–19.

6 The Forlorn Station

1. Hume, 'My Own Life', p. 10.

2. Or ulcerative colitis following on bacillary dysentery. Mossner, *Life of Hume*, p. 596.

3. *Corr*, p. 187.

4. *Corr*, p. 190.

5. To Strahan, 5 September 1776, *Corr*, p. 211.

6. *Corr*, pp. 194–5.

7. *Corr*, p. 196.

8. 'Imitative Arts', *EPS*, p. 184.

9. To Strahan, Kirkcaldy, 3 June 1776, *Corr*, pp. 196–7.

10. *Corr*, p. 201.

11. *Corr*, p. 202.

12. James Boswell, 'An Account of My Last Interview with David Hume, Esq.', Sunday, 7 July 1776, in C. McC. Weis and F. A. Pottle (eds.), *Boswell in Extremes*, London, 1971, p. 12.

13. Weis and Pottle, *Boswell in Extremes*, p. xviii.

14. To John Home, 16 July 1776, in G. Streminger, *David Hume: Sein Leben und sein Werk*, Paderborn, 1994, p. 651.

15. *Corr*, pp. 203–4.

16. *Corr*, p. 206.

17. *Corr*, p. 207.

18. *Corr*, p. 208.

19. *Corr*, p. 209.

20. *Corr*, p. 216.

21. 'Such, Echecrates, was the end of our companion, a man who, we may fairly state, was of all those we knew in our time the most virtuous, and on the whole the wisest and most just.' *Phaedo*, 118.

22. *Corr*, p. 221.

23. 'Since [his] absurd eulogium on Hume, and his ignorant, ungrateful attack on the English University education, I have no desire to be much with him.' *Journal*, 14 September 1779, in C. N. Fifer (ed.), *The Correspondence of James Boswell with Certain Members of the Club*, London, 1776, p. xc. Boswell, of course, had been at college in Scotland.

24. *Corr*, p. 251.

25. *Corr*, p. 228.

26. To Strahan, Kirkcaldy, 14 January 1778, *Corr*, p. 231.

27. *Corr*, pp. 252–3.

28. W. Smellie, 'Life of Smith', *Literary and Characteristical Lives*, Edinburgh, 1800, p. 297.

29. *Corr*, Appendix D.

30. To Lord Carlisle, Edinburgh, 8 November 1779, *Corr*, p. 242.

31. Edinburgh, 1 November 1779, *Corr*, p. 241.

32. Edinburgh, 3 January 1780, *Corr*, p. 246.

33. *WN*, p. 825.

34. *Corr*, pp. 245–6.

35. Edinburgh, 14 October 1782, *Corr*, p. 262.

36. *The Correspondence of Sir John Sinclair, Bart.*, London, 1831, Vol. 1, pp. 390–91.

37. Smellie, *Characteristical Lives*, p. 296.

38. From 'A True Account of the Behaviour and Conduct of Archibald Stewart, Esq., Late Lord Provost of Edinburgh', Edinburgh, 1746, which was attributed by Sir Walter Scott to Hume. It does not read like Hume.

39. Smellie, *Characteristical Lives*, p. 296.

40. Walter Scott, 'Life and Works of John Home', in *Essays on Chivalry, Romance and the Drama*, London, 1888, p. 388. Robert Chambers, in *Traditions of Edinburgh*, Edinburgh, c.1910, p. 319, locates the story at Panmure House and the lady as Jeanie Douglas.

41. Scott, 'Life and Works of Home', in *Essays on Chivalry*, p. 388.

42. *Corr*, p. 321.

43. 'Un de ceux que je vis le plus souvent; il me combla de politesse et chercha à me procurer tous les objects d'instruction.' Barthélemy Faujus de Saint-Fond, *Voyage en Angleterre, en Ecosse, et aux îles Hébrides*, Paris, 1797, Vol. 2, p. 278.

44. *LJ*, p. 336.

45. Stewart, 'Life of Smith', *EPS*, p. 305.

46. Smellie, *Characteristical Lives*, p. 293.

47. James Hutton, *Abstract of a Dissertation read in the Royal Society of Edinburgh upon the Seventh of March, and Fourth of April, 1785, concerning the System of the Earth, its Duration, and Stability*, reprinted, Edinburgh, 1997, p. 19.

48. James Hutton, *Theory of the Earth with Proofs and Illustrations*, Vol. 2, Edinburgh, 1795, p. 562.

49. *Corr*, p. 247.

50. *Corr*, p. 263.

51. Stewart, 'Life of Smith', *EPS*, p. 326.

52. *Corr*, p. 265.

53. To Strahan, Edinburgh, 6 October 1783, *Corr*, p. 269.

54. Edinburgh, 10 June 1784, *Corr*, p. 275.

55. *WN*, 'The Text and Apparatus', p. 62.

56. *WN*, p. 570. Bolts had written: 'Monopolies of all kinds are in their natures unavoidably pernicious; but an absolute government of monopolists, such as at present that of Bengal in fact is, must of all be the most dreadful.' William Bolts, *Considerations on India Affairs*, London, 1772 (2nd edn), p. vi.

57. Henry Mackenzie, *Works*, Vol 7, Edinburgh, 1808, p. 257; *WN*, pp. 495–6.

58. To le duc de La Rochefoucauld, Edinburgh, 1 November 1785, *Corr*, pp. 286–7.

59. India Board, 21 March 1787, *Corr*, p. 303.

60. John Kay, *A Series of Original Portraits*, Edinburgh, 1838, p. 75; Rae, *Life*, p. 405.

61. *Corr*, pp. 308–9.
62. *Corr*, p. 311.
63. *Corr*, p. 432.
64. *Corr*, p. 315.
65. *Corr*, p. 432.
66. To Robert Graham, Ellisland, 13 May 1789, *Letters of Robert Burns*, Vol. 1, ed. J. Ferguson, Oxford, 1931, p. 335.
67. To Cadell, Edinburgh, 31 March 1789, *Corr*, p. 320.
68. Edinburgh, 25 March 1789, *Corr*, p. 318.
69. P. W. Clayden, *The Early Life of Samuel Rogers*, London, 1887, p. 96.
70. Heiner Klemme, 'Adam Smith an Thomas Cadell: Zwei neue Briefe', *Archiv für Geschichte der Philosophie*, Vol. 73, 1991, pp. 277–80.
71. *TMS*, p. 91.
72. *TMS*, p. 61.
73. *TMS*, p. 63.
74. *TMS*, pp. 212–13.
75. *TMS*, pp. 230–33. Smith attributes the phrase 'divine maxim' to Cicero, but it is his own. Plato's maxim is at *Crito*, 51c: 'Violence to your parents is a sin, but violence against your country is a far greater sin.'
76. *TMS*, pp. 235–7.
77. To Robert Cullen, Edinburgh, 9 February 1790, *Corr*, p. 323.
78. Edinburgh, 25 May 1790, *Corr*, p. 325.
79. Smellie, *Memoirs*, Vol. 1, p. 295.
80. Stewart, 'Life of Smith', *EPS*, p. 328n.

81. 'It is but seldom that a philosopher ... succeeds completely to his wish in stating to others, the grounds upon which his own opinions are founded ... An apprehension that, by not doing justice to an important argument, the progress of truth may be rather retarded than advanced, have probably induced many authors to withhold from the world the unfinished results of their most valuable labours.' Stewart, 'Life of Smith', *EPS*, p. 327.

82. Clayden, *Early Life of Rogers*, p. 168.

83. Stewart, 'Life of Smith', *EPS*, p. 327n.

84. Clayden, *Early Life of Rogers*, p. 168.

85. Stewart, 'Life of Smith', *EPS*, p. 328n.

Index

Index